WHAT'S A GIRL TO DO?

finding faith
in everyday life

Other books in the growing Faithgirlz!™ library:

NIV The Faithgirlz! Bible
NIV Faithgirlz! Backpack Bible
My Faithgirlz! Journal

Nonfiction

No Boys Allowed: Devotions for Girls
Girlz Rock: Devotions for You
Chick Chat: More Devotions for Girls
Shine On, Girl!: Devotions to Keep You Sparkling

Check out www.faithgirlz.com

faiThGirLz!™

WHAT'S A GIRL TO DO?

finding faith in everyday life

by kristi holl

ZONDERkidz™

ZONDERVAN.com/
AUTHORTRACKER
follow your favorite authors

So we fix our eyes not on what is seen, but on what
is unseen. For what is seen is temporary, but what is
unseen is eternal.

—2 Corinthians 4:18

What's a Girl to Do?
Copyright © 2007 by Kristi Holl

Requests for information should be addressed to:
Zonderkidz, Grand Rapids, Michigan 49530

Library of Congress Cataloging-in-Publication Data
Holl, Kristi.
    What's a girl to do? : finding faith in everyday life / by Kristi Holl.
       p. cm. -- (Faithgirlz!)
    ISBN-13: 978-0-310-71348-7 (softcover)
    ISBN-10: 0-310-71348-X (softcover)
    1. Girls--Prayers and devotions--Juvenile literature. 2. Girls--Religious life--Juvenile
literature. 3. Girls--Conduct of life--Juvenile literature. I. Title.
    BV4860.H637 2007
    248.8'2--dc22

             2007022892

Editor: Barbara Scott
Interior Design: Christine Orejuela-Winkelman
Art Direction: Merit Alderink

Printed in the United States of America

07 08 09 10 11 12 13 14 • 14 13 12 11 10 9 8 7 6 5 4 3 2 1

TABLE OF CONTENTS

FROM INDIFFERENCE ...

The poor are shunned by all their relatives—how much more do their friends avoid them! Though they pursue them with pleading, they are nowhere to be found.

—Proverbs 19:7 (TNIV)

Elizabeth raked leaves for an elderly lady in the neighborhood. She liked the wages, but she felt uncomfortable when Mrs. Krauss came out on the porch to talk. Elizabeth said hello but continued raking while Mrs. Kraus talked or asked her to sit on the porch and have a cookie or lemonade. Elizabeth wanted to finish raking and get back home where she could call a friend or do her own thing. Elizabeth's mom said Mrs. Krauss was lonely after losing her husband. While Elizabeth pitied her neighbor, she wished she didn't have to spend her time helping her.

Showing indifference toward people shows that you don't value them very much. Indifferent people don't notice or pay attention to the needs of others. They are usually too busy concentrating on themselves.

The next time Mrs. Krauss invited Elizabeth to sit and have a cookie, Elizabeth said, "Thanks, but I'm really busy today." When she left, Elizabeth waved and called, "I'll join you another time, Mrs. Krauss!" Mrs. Krauss nodded and waved. But Elizabeth could tell she was disappointed.

Elizabeth's cheery words don't help. Good intentions don't help either, unless you follow through. Think about how a young woman can grow from being indifferent to showing her soft heart of compassion.

WHAT'S A GIRL TO DO?

Which girl seems to be showing indifference?

☐ When she sees the red Salvation Army bucket, Cassie reaches into her purse for a dollar. She smiles shyly at the bell ringer, drops in her dollar, and hurries into the warm store.

☐ When Becky hears about children who survived a flood, she decides to organize a clothes-and-toys drive at school. After a month, the school has enough to deliver ten boxes to the local shelter.

☐ When she is walking down the street, Kayla skips right by several homeless people while she tells funny stories to her friends.

CONNECTING TO GOD

Lord, please help me to see ways that I can be more like Christ and help others in need. Your love is so amazing. Amen.

more to explore

If any one of you has material possessions and sees a brother or sister in need but has no pity on them, how can the love of God be in you?

—1 John 3:17 (TNIV)

... TO COMPASSION

**Dear children, let's not merely say that we love each
other; let us show the truth by our actions.**

—1 John 3:18 (NLT)

One Saturday morning you watch your neighbor across the
street struggle into her house, juggling bags of groceries, a
baby, and a toddler. While she is trying to calm the wailing
baby, a grocery sack rips open and spills its contents on the
ground. The toddler runs toward the street with the young
mom in pursuit, carrying the wailing baby. You feel really
sorry for the young woman. How does she handle that every
day? It would drive you crazy! Just watching her makes you
feel overwhelmed. You want to say something encouraging,
but you don't want to embarrass her or say the wrong thing.

A person with compassion feels sympathy toward
another person's problem but also wants to help in a real
way. We often say that we care about others—we may
even believe it—but until our words turn into actions, we're
not helping. If you see someone in trouble, help in the way
you'd like to be helped if you were in the same situation.
Don't let embarrassment stop you from volunteering your
services.

Based on what you observed, you make a decision.
Early the following Saturday morning, you ring the young

woman's doorbell. You introduce yourself and offer to babysit so she can go grocery shopping alone. The mother looks astonished at first, then grins and hugs you. "You're an angel!" she cries. You blink in surprise, smile back, and start making a plan with her.

WHAT'S A GIRL TO DO?

Which girl seems to be showing compassion?

☐ On her way to class, Libby noticed her friend standing in front of her locker looking overwhelmed. Libby squeezed her friend's arm and said, "Let's walk to class together."

☐ Mira's mom was tired when she came home from work. Mira noticed that her mom seemed busy, but she said, "When are we going to eat?"

☐ Rose was jumping rope with two good friends. She thought about inviting a new girl to join them, but thought it might mess up the balance of the game they were playing.

CONNECTING TO GOD

Lord, I want to be more aware of others. If someone has a need, show me how to take positive action to help. Amen.

more to explore

Carry each other's burdens, and in this way you will fulfill the law of Christ.

—Galatians 6:2 (TNIV)

FROM RASHNESS . . .

> **It is not good to have zeal without knowledge, nor to
> be hasty and miss the way.**
>
> —Proverbs 19:2

Sara was starving after school, and there was nothing
decent to eat but a frozen pizza. She would need to cut it
in half to make it fit in the toaster oven, but Sara wasn't
allowed to use a sharp knife when her mom wasn't home.
Sara thought briefly about the house rule—then her stomach growled. Sara grabbed the sharp knife, intending to use
it, clean it, and put it back. Instead, the knife slipped as she
hacked through the pizza. She cut herself badly.

To be *rash* means "to do things in a hurry," usually
without thinking or praying first. Eagerness without common
sense isn't helpful. A girl who rushes to act can make bad
decisions—with even worse consequences. In the end,
she'll fail to meet her goal (in Sara's case, eating pizza) and
cause herself additional trouble (Sara's injured hand).

Sara was rash. She didn't think before she acted. What
facts did she ignore? First, her mom had told her not to
use the knives. God's Word says, "Children, obey your
parents in everything, for this pleases the Lord" (Colossians 3:20). Second, she forgot that knives can slip and cut

you—badly. Third, she ignored the fact that if caught, she'd be in big trouble. Being hasty in your actions never pays, but there's a better way. A girl can grow from being rash to showing sensible caution.

WHAT'S A GIRL TO DO?

Which girl is showing the trait of rashness?

☐ Kayla is babysitting when she sees a boy she likes pedaling by on his bike. She leaves the child alone and runs outside to chat.

☐ Libby goes shopping for a Mother's Day card and sees a clearance rack of T-shirts. She really wants a T-shirt, but she checks her wallet and just buys a beautiful card.

☐ Cassie is walking home from school when a driver (unknown to her) offers her a ride. She says, "No, thanks" and keeps walking.

CONNECTING TO GOD

Dear Lord, help me take time to think and pray before acting. I want to make good decisions. Amen.

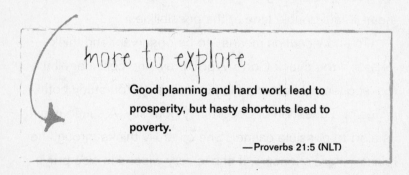

more to explore

Good planning and hard work lead to prosperity, but hasty shortcuts lead to poverty.

—Proverbs 21:5 (NLT)

... TO CAUTION

The simple believe anything, but the prudent give thought to their steps.

—Proverbs 14:15 (TNIV)

You eagerly read an email from someone who is arriving in your town next month to audition middle-school students for acting in commercials. You've always wanted to be an actress. If you could earn money making commercials, you could pay for the summer acting lessons you long to take. You read the email again. It sounds honest. The ad says where to go for the audition, and you're fairly certain where the building is located. Won't your family and friends be amazed when you land a TV spot? You have to send the $25 registration fee within a week to the out-of-state address given, and you'll be added to the audition list. Your heart beats double time at the possibilities.

To show *caution* means "to be observant and think ahead." You check God's Word, pray, and consider all the consequences before acting or deciding. You study both sides of a question or opportunity honestly. A cautious girl is alert to possible danger. She carefully thinks through her plans before choosing. If she is very wise, she also prays and asks the Lord for direction.

In the end, you decide not to respond to the email on your own. Instead, you tell your parents about it during supper. Together you prepare a response, asking for more facts and proof that the person actually owns and runs a real talent company. You never hear another word from the talent scout. The talent company never comes to town either—and you keep your $25!

WHAT'S A GIRL TO DO?

Which girls are showing the trait of caution?

- ☐ Rose unplugs the toaster before poking a fork inside to dislodge her bagel.
- ☐ Becky answers the door without checking the peephole because she knows it has to be the pizza delivery guy.
- ☐ Mira notices the icy sidewalk and changes into shoes with rubber soles and good traction.

CONNECTING TO GOD

Lord, I want to be careful and alert in all situations. Show me what to believe and help me plan my way. Amen.

more to explore

The prudent understand where they are going, but fools deceive themselves.

—Proverbs 14:8 (NLT)

FROM LYING . . .

Save me, Lord, from lying lips and from deceitful tongues.

—Psalm 120:2 (TNIV)

Jamie lived alone with her dad for three years after her mom died. She had a lot of freedom, so when he remarried, it was a huge adjustment. Jamie knew she needed to talk to her dad about her feelings, but she put it off. Instead, Jamie dragged her feet on the way home every day, reluctant to spend time alone with her stepmom after school. Several days a week, Jamie took a detour on the way home—sometimes to the local mall, other times to hang out at friends' houses. Jamie told her stepmom she was doing research in the library for a school project. She didn't feel guilty about lying; after all, she wasn't going anywhere bad. "Anyway," Jamie reasoned, "what she doesn't know won't hurt her."

A lying person is someone who purposely gives incorrect information. She withholds information or doesn't tell the truth. A liar sometimes calls her stories "white lies" or "fibs" or "shading the truth." But God's Word calls it being dishonest, or deceitful.

Jamie's dad eventually confronted her about the extra hours after school, demanding to see the reports and projects she was working on. The truth came out. Jamie lost some privileges and—even worse—her family's trust. She learned that lying—even "innocent untruths"—had big consequences. After that, her dad and stepmom talked to her about her feelings of disappointment.

WHAT'S A GIRL TO DO?

Which girls are practicing the trait of lying?

- ☐ Mira started cleaning her room, but shoved most of the mess under the bed. She told her dad she was done so she could get her allowance.
- ☐ Rose is asked to a party she doesn't want to attend. She says, "Thanks, but I have other plans that night." (Those plans include staying home and watching TV with her little sister.)
- ☐ Becky tells her teacher she forgot her math at home, but she doesn't mention that she didn't finish it.

CONNECTING TO GOD

Dear Lord, I want to be honest 24/7. Help me when I'm tempted to lie—no matter how small the lie. Amen.

more to explore

My God, whom I praise, do not remain silent, for people who are wicked and deceitful have opened their mouths against me; they have spoken against me with lying tongues.
—Psalm 109:1–2 (TNIV)

... TO HONESTY

Each of you must put off falsehood and speak truthfully to your neighbor, for we are all members of one body.

—Ephesians 4:25 (TNIV)

You're sitting in the theater with your whole family, enjoying a movie that you've eagerly awaited for nearly a year. Your eyes are glued to the action on the screen. It's every bit as good as the previews and early publicity promised. During one electrifying scene, your first-grade sister tugs on your arm. "I have to go to the bathroom," she whispers urgently. "Do you know where it is?" Rolling your eyes, you're tempted to answer, *I have no clue. Ask Mom to take you.* You glance down the row at your mom, who's enjoying the movie just as much as you are. You sigh and say, "I know where it is. I'll take you."

Honesty simply means you "tell the truth." You are straightforward—someone who can be trusted. You don't tell half-truths or try to mislead people. Honesty can be kind and gentle or blunt, even cruel. Godly honesty is truth spoken with love and understanding.

Sometimes it's hard to be honest. Telling the truth might mean you'll get into trouble, like being honest about breaking a window. Or it can mean extra work: "Yes, I have time to do that for you." God's Word commands that we tell the truth, even when it's hard. If you do, you'll please your heavenly Father and gain a reputation for integrity—both huge rewards!

WHAT'S A GIRL TO DO?

Which girl is showing the trait of honesty?

- ☐ Kayla leaves her homework on the bus, but when she explains to the teacher, she also admits it wasn't quite finished.
- ☐ Cassie doesn't like her friend's new hairstyle but says, "I've never seen anything so perfect! I want to get mine cut just like it!"
- ☐ Libby stays late after school helping a friend. This makes her late for soccer practice, and she tells the coach her teacher kept her late at school.

CONNECTING TO GOD

Dear Lord, I want to be honest and truthful with each person in my life, but it's hard. Please give me the courage I need. Amen.

more to explore

I speak the truth in Christ—I am not lying, my conscience confirms it through the Holy Spirit.

—Romans 9:1 (TNIV)

**Your beauty should not come from outward adorn-
ment, such as elaborate hairstyles and the wearing of
gold jewelry and fine clothes.**

—1 Peter 3:3 (TNIV)

Laci loved to roller-skate. She could skate forward, back-
ward, and in pairs. When she arrived at the roller rink, she
glanced around to see who was there. She wanted to see if
Chad was there. Then she spotted him. Chad was skating
with Brittney, who was dressed in skintight, low-cut jeans
and a tube top that showed her tan stomach to perfection.
Laci glanced down at her own outfit: baggy jeans and her
favorite tie-dyed T-shirt. Now it looked babyish to her. *If only
I could dress like Brittney*, Laci thought. *Then I'd get my
share of attention*. But Laci's parents would never allow it.

Worldly beauty is what Hollywood and fashion maga-
zines define as beauty. It is dressing for attention. Today's
worldly standards of beauty often include extreme thinness
and skimpy clothing. God's Word tells us a beautiful woman
is much more than the clothing she wears.

Laci also spotted Kaitlyn, a girl from her class. She
had pimples on her face, and her faded jeans and T-shirt
appeared old, but she obviously didn't care. Neither did her
friends. Kaitlyn laughed and talked, surrounded by a group

of girls and guys. Her cheerful eyes—and her friendly smile—made her pretty.

WHAT'S A GIRL TO DO?

Which girl is too concerned about worldly beauty?

☐ Kayla gets a handmade sweater from her grandma. She doesn't really like the color, but she loves that her grandma made it just for her. She wears it right away.

☐ Cassie gets out of bed and pulls out her favorite jeans and T-shirt. She likes the invisible feeling she has when she is wearing these clothes.

☐ Becky doesn't have enough money for a pair of designer-label jeans, so she charges them on her mom's credit card rather than buying what she can afford.

CONNECTING TO GOD

Lord, forgive me for envying others who dress for attention. Help me love who I am. Amen.

more to explore

[Women] should wear decent and appropriate clothing and not draw attention to themselves by the way they fix their hair or by wearing gold or pearls or expensive clothes. For women who claim to be devoted to God should make themselves attractive by the good things they do.

—1 Timothy 2:9–10 (NLT)

... TO SELF-ACCEPTANCE

**Rather, [your beauty] should be that of your inner self,
the unfading beauty of a gentle and quiet spirit, which
is of great worth in God's sight.**

—1 Peter 3:4 (TNIV)

You notice your friends are talking more about their looks.
One friend hates her curly hair. Another friend worries that
she's fat. When you enter middle school, you decide to
focus on something far more valuable instead. You try to be
as kind and friendly as possible.

Self-acceptance is a satisfaction with who you are and
how you look. For a Christian, it is knowing that God made
you just the way you are for a reason—and that you're
truly beautiful in God's eyes. It is confidence that being
who you were truly meant to be is more becoming than any
clothing you could wear. "The LORD does not look at the
things human beings look at. People look at the outward
appearance, but the LORD looks at the heart" (1 Samuel
16:7 TNIV). A girl with self-acceptance chooses clothes
she personally loves and feels good in—regardless of
what's in fashion. If pink and orange jackets are "in" this
year, but you love jean jackets instead, wear your old denim
one! Be happy with your own preferences. Don't let the
fashion world dictate your choices for you.

Studies have shown that when people are asked what traits they value in a friend, "good looks" are rarely mentioned. Traits like loyalty, kindness, a good smile, a sense of humor, and being fun rank *much* higher than physical appearance. So don't buy into the world's values that focus on body build, beauty, clothes, and jewelry. Focus instead on being beautiful according to God's standards—then you'll be beautiful inside *and* out.

WHAT'S A GIRL TO DO?

Which girl is showing the trait of self-acceptance?

- ☐ Libby throws away her favorite kitten sweater after someone laughs at it.
- ☐ Even though she has been told she is a klutz, Rose joins a ballet class because she loves the idea of moving with the music.
- ☐ Cassie decides to fast for three days before try-outs. She thinks she has to be skinny to get the lead part in the school play.

CONNECTING TO GOD

Lord, please help me ignore what the world says about beauty. I want to be beautiful *inside*, where it counts. Amen.

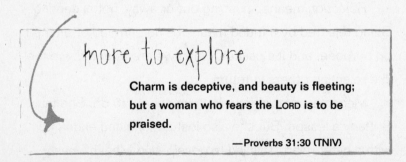

more to explore

Charm is deceptive, and beauty is fleeting; but a woman who fears the Lord is to be praised.
—Proverbs 31:30 (TNIV)

FROM REJECTION . . .

When they hurled their insults at him, he did not retaliate; when he suffered, he made no threats.

—1 Peter 2:23 (TNIV)

Megan and Brittany were paired on their science fair project. On Friday afternoon, Megan invited Brittany to come over for pizza that night before working on their project. "Sorry, I can't," Brittany said. "My grandma's coming for dinner, and I need to be home." Megan was disappointed, but she understood. That night, when she went with her dad to pick up a carryout pizza, she spotted Brittany sitting in a booth with Lindsay. They were laughing and eating pizza, and they didn't see her. Megan felt the painful stab of rejection. On Monday, Brittany was friendly as usual, but Megan was cold and silent as they worked on their project. *Brittany deserves to see how rejection feels*, Megan thought.

Rejection means "pushing out or away, not accepting." Being rejected by a friend means being dumped or ditched on purpose, and it's painful. When we are rejected, we feel like rejecting others in return.

Megan accomplished what she set out to do. She taught Brittany a lesson. But she also lost a friend and ended up with a bitter heart. This led to gossip, and Megan's nasty comments got back to Brittany. An all-out war erupted. Rejecting someone back might feel good for the moment, but it causes long-term trouble. There's a better way!

WHAT'S A GIRL TO DO?

Which girl is rejecting a friend?

- ☐ When Nancy invites her over after school, Becky tells her she can't come today because she has too much homework, but she might be able to come tomorrow.
- ☐ Mira cries when she isn't invited to Missy's party and then rents a favorite DVD for that evening.
- ☐ Kayla is upset when her two best friends join soccer as buddies, so she ignores them at school to punish them.

CONNECTING TO GOD

Lord, thank you for never rejecting *me*. When I feel left out, help me not to reject others back. Amen.

more to explore

Love your enemies, do good to them, and lend to them without expecting to get anything back. Then your reward will be great, and you will be children of the Most High, because he is kind to the ungrateful and wicked.

—Luke 6:35 (TNIV)

... TO FORGIVENESS

Make allowance for each other's faults, and forgive anyone who offends you. Remember, the Lord forgave you, so you must forgive others.

—Colossians 3:13 (NLT)

For Culture Day at school, you plan a cooking display to make your grandmother's German caramel candy. Your friends will love the samples, and you'll get an A for sure. Your best friend, Emily, agrees that it's a cool idea. On Culture Day, you arrive early to set up your booth. Emily is already there, making Korean candy to give away. You fume while you work. Now it looks like you've copied Emily—when the candy giveaway was *your* idea! Gritting your teeth, you decide to avoid Emily all day. After fifteen minutes of anger, you realize you miss goofing around with your best friend.

Forgiveness means "to give up ideas of revenge or making the other person pay." God's Word says that we are to forgive the person who offends or hurts us. God forgave us, so we must forgive others.

In the end, you decide to forgive Emily and stop avoiding her. It wasn't right for Emily to steal your idea, but you make a choice to let it go and stop "paying Emily back." You pray to God for strength to say the right thing to Emily.

Then you tell Emily how you feel. She says she is sorry, and, surprisingly, when you give up the anger, your natural joy floods back.

WHAT'S A GIRL TO DO?

Which girl is showing forgiveness?

☐ The child pushing the cart behind Mira in the grocery checkout bangs into her leg painfully. She wants to yell, "Watch it, twerp!" but she says nothing and lets it go.

☐ Cassie discovers that her sister has borrowed her sweater without permission, so she storms into her sister's room and takes something of *hers* without asking.

☐ Rose is reading in a lawn chair outside. Her brother is playing noisily next to her and won't leave her alone. She keeps yelling at him to stop, but nothing changes.

CONNECTING TO GOD

Dear Lord, thank you for always forgiving me. Please help me to really forgive others and put my forgiveness into action. Amen.

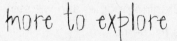

more to explore

Forgive us our sins, as we have forgiven those who sin against us.

—Matthew 6:12 (NLT)

From DISCOURAGING ...

"Why do you discourage the Israelites from crossing over into the land the LORD has given them?"
—Numbers 32:7 (TNIV)

Emma's youth group wanted to raise several hundred dollars for a short mission trip into a neighboring state. Aaron, a boy in her group, suggested several ways they could earn the money. They could have a car wash or a bake sale or do yard work for church members. Emma snickered with her friends and then raised her hand. "There's no way you'll see me doing any of those things. Those ideas are, like, so *old-fashioned*. Nobody bakes anymore. And it's ninety degrees in the shade! Who's going to do yard work? You want us to keel over with a heatstroke?" Aaron's smile faded, and he offered no further suggestions.

Discouraging means "dampening someone's spirits or enthusiasm." Discouraging people are like a bucket of cold water tossed on a flickering fire. A discouraging person dashes people's hopes, deflating ideas and dreams. After a while, we avoid discouraging people, and we stop confiding our dreams and hopes to them.

When making decisions—about raising money or anything else—it's always a good plan to look at both sides of an idea. But you can talk about the pros and cons of a plan without discouraging someone from moving ahead or try-ing something new. Next time someone presents an idea, hold your tongue and avoid making discouraging remarks. Instead, your goal should be to *first* point out positive things about the plan.

WHAT'S A GIRL TO DO?

Which girls are showing the trait of being discouraging?

- ☐ When Kayla and her language arts team work on their poster together, Kayla points out the others' mistakes in order to be "helpful" and have the best poster in the class.
- ☐ Mira looks at her younger brother's spelling test and asks, "Why did you miss so many easy words?"
- ☐ Becky realizes that her grandpa isn't hearing so well anymore, but she decides not to mention it and just talks louder.

CONNECTING TO GOD

Dear Lord, thank you for always encouraging me when I need it. Help me never to discourage others. Amen.

more to explore

The peoples around them set out to discour-age the people of Judah and make them afraid to go on building.

—Ezra 4:4 (TNIV)

We sent Timothy ... to strengthen and encourage you in your faith.

—1 Thessalonians 3:2 (TNIV)

You're bundled up against the wind-driven snow as you hurry onto school grounds. Peering over the scarf wrapped around your face, you're glad to see Mr. Thomkins, the custodian, out front scooping a path through the drifting snow. The sidewalks are a block long, and the snow drifts over them even as he scoops. You hurry past him, calling, "Hey, Mr. Thomkins!" He nods, never missing a beat with the snow shovel. As you open the door to the warm building, you stop ... and then go back. You reach into your pocket for the chocolate-chip granola bar you were saving for after school. "You'll need this!" you shout to him. "Thanks for doing such a great job. We appreciate you." Mr. Thomkins takes the granola bar and grins. When you head inside, you notice he is scooping with increased vigor.

Uplifting means "raising someone's spirits or inspiring someone to action." An uplifting person encourages others, helping them to do even better. Uplifting people are a joy to be around! They can help turn tired, discouraged people into energized, hopeful individuals.

As a follower of Jesus, you should be on the lookout for discouraged, downcast, and tired people. It might even be your mother or little brother! Stop and give them an uplifting word or maybe a hug. We all need encouragement from time to time. Lighten someone's load today with an inspiring word.

WHAT'S A GIRL TO DO?

Which girl is showing the trait of being uplifting?

- ☐ Libby sees a classmate trying to fix the tetherball that came off the rope, again. Libby calls out, "Don't even bother. You won't be able to fix it."
- ☐ Becky's sister is trying to figure out the directions for folding an origami crane. Becky walks by without saying anything.
- ☐ While Cassie's brother struggles to memorize a poem for school, Cassie says, "Just take it one line at a time—I know you can do it!"

CONNECTING TO GOD

Dear Lord, thank you for lifting me up so many times when I was down. Please help me to see the needs of others and do the same. Amen.

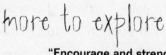

more to explore

"Encourage and strengthen [Joshua], for he will lead this people across and will cause them to inherit the land that you will see."
—Deuteronomy 3:28 (TNIV)

FROM UNREASONABLE ...

> "We are given no straw, but the slave drivers still demand, 'Make bricks!' We are being beaten, but it isn't our fault! Your own people are to blame."
> —Exodus 5:16 (NLT)

Samantha stood on the front steps, tapping her foot impatiently. Where was that big sister of hers? Marla knew Samantha wanted to go to the mall tonight! *If I had a driver's license, I wouldn't have to wait for a ride with her*, Sam thought. She shifted her load of books to the other arm. If her sister didn't hurry, Sam wouldn't have time to shop after returning her library books. Finally, Marla's car turned into the driveway. Samantha ran to the passenger side and climbed in. "Where have you *been*?" she demanded. Her sweaty sister, still in damp shorts and T-shirt, replied, "I had track practice after school, remember? I'm starving." Samantha slammed the door and fastened her seat belt. "No time to eat. Let's go," she said.

Being *unreasonable* means "expecting or asking for things that aren't justified, thoughtful, or fair." Unreasonable demands are often made by people who don't take into account all the facts — or other people's needs.

Samantha had a plan that involved her sister's help. Although Samantha had legitimate needs, so did her sister.

Samantha expected her sister to do all the sacrificing. It would have been more sensible—and kinder—for Samantha to allow her sister to rest and eat before they completed Samantha's plan. Then they could go out and enjoy their time together.

WHAT'S A GIRL TO DO?

Which girl is showing the trait of being unreasonable?

- ◯ Mira leaves for school fifteen minutes late and is angry at her homeroom teacher because she marks her tardy.
- ◯ Cassie decides to wait until after supper to ask her dad for help with her homework because she sees that he is busy.
- ◯ After a busy day, Rose needs some quiet time in her room. Her brother asks her to play a game, but she tells him she wants to read for an hour first.

CONNECTING TO GOD

Dear Lord, I don't want to be unreasonable. Help me to think first and make sensible, fair decisions. Amen.

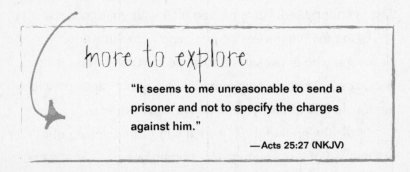

more to explore

"It seems to me unreasonable to send a prisoner and not to specify the charges against him."

—Acts 25:27 (NKJV)

... TO FAIR

> "Yet you say, 'The way of the Lord is not fair.' Hear
> now, O house of Israel, is it not My way which is fair,
> and your ways which are not fair?"
>
> —Ezekiel 18:25 (NKJV)

Your parents have a rule that you must sit with them during church, but they let you invite your best friend, Nina, to sit with you. You and Nina are as close as sisters, even though you attend different schools and see each other only on Sundays. One Sunday she says she can't sit with you because her cousins are visiting, and she needs to sit with them. You're hurt and angry for a minute, wondering why Nina doesn't invite you to join them. Then you remember that Nina knows your family's rule and probably thinks there's no point in asking you. You choose to smile and say, "I understand. Have a good time with your cousins."

Being *fair* means "to be just" and not take sides. Someone who is fair listens to all points of view and isn't prejudiced. A fair person is reasonable about other people's needs instead of always demanding her own way.

Often, being fair goes hand in hand with thinking of others instead of just yourself. We sometimes cry, "That's not fair!" when in truth we mean, "I want my way!" Thinking carefully before speaking is one good way to help yourself change from being unreasonable to being fair.

WHAT'S A GIRL TO DO?

Which girls are showing the trait of fairness?

☐ Libby and her brother want the same cereal for breakfast, but there isn't much left. Libby pours the rest of the cereal into two bowls. Then she lets her brother choose which bowl he wants.

☐ Becky wants to IM her friend before bedtime, but her sister needs to type a paper that is due the next day. Becky lets her sister use the computer instead.

☐ Kayla gets her homework done early one day. Her brother needs help with his math homework, but Kayla doesn't want to give up her computer time to help him.

CONNECTING TO GOD

Dear Lord, thank you for always being fair with me. Help me to be fair when I deal with others. Amen.

more to explore

If a king judges the poor with fairness, his throne will be established forever.
—Proverbs 29:14 (TNIV)

The prudent keep their knowledge to themselves,
but a fool's heart blurts out folly.

—Proverbs 12:23 (TNIV)

Taylor wanted to get her mom a CD of her favorite band for Christmas. Her mom would love it! Taylor had enough money, but every time she tried to make it to the music store, something came up. Her dad offered to take her several times, but Taylor was busy with homework, parties, and holiday specials on TV. When Christmas was only a few days away, Taylor begged her dad to take her to the music store. Unfortunately, when she arrived at the busy store, Taylor found that the CD was sold out and wouldn't be in stock again until January. Taylor wished she had gone to the store weeks ago.

Being *foolish* means "to be unwise in your words, choices, and actions." A foolish girl may behave and talk in ways that are careless, reckless, impulsive, and not sensible. A foolish girl doesn't stop to think before she speaks or acts.

Although Taylor had good intentions, she didn't think about the consequences of her laid-back attitude. If she had, she might have realized that the popular CD might not stay on the shelves. Foolish people don't consider the possible outcomes before acting and speaking. So they often suffer unnecessary bad consequences.

WHAT'S A GIRL TO DO?

Which girls are showing the trait of foolishness?

- [ ] Kayla reaches across three people in the booth to grab the salt and knocks over a girl's soda in the process.
- [ ] Rose is playing a game on the computer when her dad says it's time to leave for church. She replies, "No way! I'm winning; I can't stop now." Rose is promptly grounded.
- [ ] Becky follows her friends off the bus while they're talking and gets off six blocks too soon.

CONNECTING TO GOD

Dear Lord, I don't want to do foolish things. Please give me your wisdom in dealing with people. Amen.

more to explore

The wise in heart accept commands, but a chattering fool comes to ruin.
—Proverbs 10:8 (TNIV)

**The fear of the LORD is the beginning of wisdom; all
who follow his precepts have good understanding.**

—Psalm 111:10 (TNIV)

After soccer practice gets out early, your friend Rachel
invites you to her house. She lives down the street from
the soccer field. Your dad is coming to pick you up in about
fifteen minutes, but Rachel is eager to go. She says, "Just
tell Coach where you're going. When your dad comes to
pick you up, Coach can tell him where you are."

That sounds reasonable to you, but what if Coach
doesn't stick around? Your dad could get really worried
about you. You tell Rachel you can't come over now. You
ask, "Can you stay at the park and play for a while?" She
decides to head home, and you kick the ball around with
your coach until your dad shows up. A girl who is wise is
sensible and intelligent, with good understanding about
people and situations. A wise person shows good judgment
and common sense. Followers of Jesus are considered
wise when they pay attention to what God's Word teaches.

A wise girl thinks through her ideas. She doesn't act or
speak impulsively, but carefully considers possible outcomes first. Then she makes a wise decision, the decision

that will get her where she wants to go! When considering your words and actions, always ask yourself, "What would Jesus do?" You can never go wrong starting there!

WHAT'S A GIRL TO DO?

Which girls are showing the trait of wisdom?

- ☐ The basketball coach yells at Mira when she misses an easy shot in the game. She holds her tongue rather than defend herself and provoke more anger.
- ☐ Libby goes to the store without a list of supplies she needs for her science project. At the store, she can't remember what she needs and ends up buying the wrong supplies.
- ☐ When her teacher keeps her after class for talking too much, Becky decides to try harder to be quiet. In the next class period, she moves away from her chatty friends.

CONNECTING TO GOD

Dear Lord, I'm tired of paying the price for foolish words and actions. Please help me grow in wisdom and common sense. Amen.

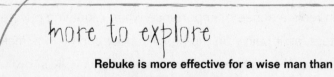

more to explore

Rebuke is more effective for a wise man than a hundred blows on a fool.

—Proverbs 17:10 (NKJV)

FROM GOSSIPY . . .

Gossips betray a confidence, but the trustworthy keep a secret.

—Proverbs 11:13 (TNIV)

Amanda was proud of the way she got along in her new blended family. People had said she'd be jealous now that she wasn't an only child anymore. But she wasn't. She actually liked her older stepsister. She loved their nightly chats. At these times, Amanda often passed along things she had overheard. Amanda had a talent for eavesdropping, and she enjoyed making her reports. She said things like, "Mom and Jack were fighting because your dad said we can't afford a vacation this summer"; and "Jack was grouchy while you were gone because he's afraid he might get fired"; and "I saw the girl next door wearing the ugliest green swimsuit you ever saw."

A gossipy girl is one who repeats stories about people—both true stories and questionable rumors. She often feels a sense of importance when repeating private matters, as if being "in the know" about such things makes her better than others. The tales she tells usually show someone in a negative light or embarrassing position. A gossip seldom checks out the truth of the stories, but instead hurriedly repeats them to others before someone can beat her to it.

Shakespeare called gossip "foul whisperings." God's Word says a gossiping tongue causes anger (Proverbs 25:23) and that gossips need something better to do with their time (1 Timothy 5:13). Instead of allowing yourself to be a gossip, be determined to be trustworthy instead!

WHAT'S A GIRL TO DO?

Which girls are showing the trait of being gossipy?

- ☐ Kayla sees Katherine's boyfriend talking to another girl, and she hurries to tell Katherine.
- ☐ Rose sees her friend's diary lying open on her bed and closes it before she can be tempted to read it.
- ☐ Mira stands behind a large classmate at the scale in the nurse's office, and she can't wait to tell others how *much* that girl weighs!

CONNECTING TO GOD

Dear Lord, thank you for pointing out when I'm about to gossip. Help me stop the flow! Amen.

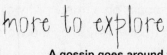

more to explore

A gossip goes around telling secrets, so don't hang around chatterers.

—Proverbs 20:19 (NLT)

... TO TRUSTWORTHY

Listen, for I have trustworthy things to say; I open my lips to speak what is right. My mouth speaks what is true, for my lips detest wickedness.

—Proverbs 8:6–7 (TNIV)

You and your cousin are spending a week at your grandma's house. Usually when you play in your grandma's attic with all the old clothes in the trunks, you both have a great time. But your cousin isn't enjoying it today, and you ask her what's wrong. After a long pause, she whispers that her grades are so low that she may flunk this year. Later, when your cousin is reading, you join Grandma outside and help weed the garden. While you work, she asks if you had fun in the attic. You'd like to discuss your cousin's secret, but you know she wants it kept private. So you talk about other subjects with Grandma instead.

To be trustworthy is to be reliable and honest, tried and true. You know you can count on a trustworthy girl. One way to tell if a person is trustworthy is by the words that come out of her mouth. Are your secrets safe with this girl? Can you trust her to be loyal? If so, you've found a treasure—a trustworthy friend.

Sometimes it can be tempting to share the secrets of others. When tempted, remember how you'd feel if someone shared a secret of *yours*. Be a girl that others can trust.

WHAT'S A GIRL TO DO?

Which girls are showing the trait of being trustworthy?

☐ Cassie borrows her friend's mp3 player and accidentally breaks the headphones. She uses her own money to replace the headphones and apologizes when she returns the player.

☐ Mira is babysitting two six-year-olds. She leaves them to play in the park while she hangs out with her friends.

☐ Libby asks her parents if she can stay home by herself for an evening. She promises to do her homework the whole time. Her parents agree because she usually does what she says she'll do.

CONNECTING TO GOD

Dear Lord, I want to be someone who can be trusted. Help me to be honest and loyal in all I do and say. Amen.

more to explore

I am about to open my mouth; my words are on the tip of my tongue. My words come from an upright heart; my lips sincerely speak what I know.

—Job 33:2–3 (TNIV)

FROM NEGATIVE ...

Why am I discouraged? Why is my heart so sad?
—Psalm 42:5 (NLT)

Brianna got called to the nurse's office after lunch because her little brother had been injured. His forehead, nose, and knees were scraped raw, and his nose looked like it might be broken. According to his teacher, he'd crawled on some forbidden construction equipment at recess and fallen off. The nurse asked Brianna to stay with him while she called their mom. Brianna sat down beside Josh. "You'll have a ripping headache for days," she said, studying his goose egg. "Mom will have a fit when she finds out how you got hurt. And you've got blood on your new shirt—it'll never come out. You might as well throw it away."

A girl with a negative attitude is pessimistic and full of doubt. This person predicts gloom and doom in most situations. Given a choice, a negative person will find fault rather than look for something good to say. Relationships with people who have negative attitudes can be exhausting.

Someone with a negative attitude may lack self-confidence. Such a person is a gloomy person to be around. If you struggle with negative thoughts, don't spread them around and bring others down. Instead, choose to make a transformation. With every word and action from now on, choose the positive response. With God's help, you can do it!

WHAT'S A GIRL TO DO?

Which girl is showing the trait of being negative?

- ☐ Cassie complains to her mom about going to Alicia's birthday party because she knows she'll have a rotten time, she doesn't have anything to wear, and Alicia won't like her present anyway.
- ☐ Rose sees the moving van pull in next door and watches them unload, keeping her hopes up that this new family will have someone she can hang out with.
- ☐ Mira studies hard, gets a good night's rest, eats a good breakfast the following morning, and heads to school. She figures she has done her best to prepare for the test.

CONNECTING TO GOD

Dear Lord, help me look for ways to be positive and hopeful. Help me to choose positive responses to people and look for the good in others. Amen.

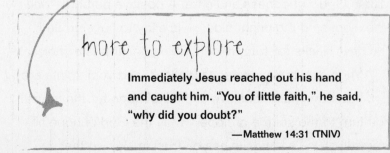

more to explore

Immediately Jesus reached out his hand and caught him. "You of little faith," he said, "why did you doubt?"

—Matthew 14:31 (TNIV)

... TO POSITIVE

As for me, I will always have hope; I will praise you more and more.

—Psalm 71:14 (TNIV)

Your music teacher broke her leg, and you have a substitute teacher for a month. You discover that the nervous sub is fresh out of college with very little teaching experience. During her first day in chorus, she stumbles over her words and has a hard time controlling the class. At the end of class, she smiles as people leave. You notice her quivering lip and suspect that she's ready to burst into tears. You stop at her desk and say, "Thanks for coming. I loved the songs you picked to sing today." You turn to leave, but not before you notice a *real* smile break out this time.

A girl who is positive has a good, constructive, helpful attitude. Such a girl is full of hope for the future, expressing faith in God's goodness and care. A positive person—one who "looks on the bright side"—is a joy to have around and never lacks for true friends. Being positive is a choice.

When circumstances seem difficult, and your spirits are low, how can you be positive and full of hope for the future? You turn to the source of hope. "May the God of hope fill you with all joy and peace as you trust in him, so that you may overflow with hope by the power of the Holy Spirit" (Romans 15:13).

WHAT'S A GIRL TO DO?

Which girls are showing the trait of being positive?

- ☐ Kayla is waiting in line at the crowded movie theater. People around her are grumpy and impatient. She smiles whenever she catches someone's eye and gives the tired person at the ticket booth a friendly greeting.
- ☐ Mira feels very hungry as she waits in the lunch line. She knows there won't be a thing she likes in today's school lunch choices.
- ☐ Becky is looking forward to her birthday party Saturday, which includes a picnic and swimming at the lake. She is sure the weather will stay fine through the weekend. But if it doesn't, they'll play games in the beach house.

CONNECTING TO GOD

Dear Lord, I want to be a positive person. Please help me remember that a positive attitude is my *choice*. Thank you for your amazing grace. Amen.

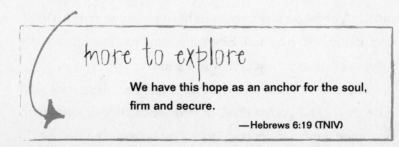

more to explore

We have this hope as an anchor for the soul, firm and secure.

—Hebrews 6:19 (TNIV)

FROM CRUEL ...

Deliver me, my God, from the hand of the wicked,
from the grasp of those who are evil and cruel.
—Psalm 71:4 (TNIV)

Morgan was mad that she had to get up and go to church
with her family. She'd been awake till four a.m. at a slumber
party, but she'd been ready when her family picked her up
on the way to Sunday school. None of Morgan's friends
had had to leave early. She'd stepped over sleeping bodies
on the way out the door. Slumped now in the church pew,
she felt annoyed by her little sister. When Jenna placed her
shepherd painting under Morgan's nose, Morgan shoved it
away. "When did you make that ugly thing?" she muttered.
"Looks like a monkey painted it. Dump it in the garbage
before it makes Mom throw up." Jenna's eyes opened
wide, then filled with tears at the cruel remarks.

A girl who is cruel is mean, sometimes even vicious and
brutal. A cruel person seems to have no heart and can look
and sound cold-blooded. She often runs roughshod (force-
fully) over others to get what she wants.

There is no excuse to *ever* be cruel. You might think you
have the right if you're tired, or your sibling is extra irritating,
or something bad happened to you at school. But *no one*

has the right to be mean and vicious. It's what the Bible calls wicked and evil. Damage done by a cruel person lasts a long time. Instead of being heartless, let God transform you into someone with a kind and generous spirit.

WHAT'S A GIRL TO DO?

Which girls are showing the trait of cruelty?

- ☐ Lydia laughs from the backseat of the car at a toothless, homeless older man.
- ☐ Caroline tells a girl in her math class to "get over it" because divorce is common and "no big deal."
- ☐ Rose sees a puppy loose in her neighborhood and ties it up with a leash until she can find its owner.

CONNECTING TO GOD

Dear Lord, forgive me for any cruel remarks I've made to others. I don't want to be that way to anyone, not ever. Amen.

---

more to explore

Anger is cruel and fury overwhelming.
—Proverbs 27:4 (TNIV)

Be kind and compassionate to one another, forgiving each other, just as in Christ God forgave you.
—Ephesians 4:32 (TNIV)

You and your friend like to take a shortcut through the city park on your way home from school. It's a shady place to stroll and a private spot to catch up on important stuff from the day. Today you are climbing near the top of the main path when suddenly two skateboarders appear over the top of the hill. The skateboarders yell at you to get out of the way. You jump out of their path, but your friend is hit and knocked down. The skateboarders keep on going. Your friend's hands are scraped and bleeding; when she stands, her foot and ankle are already swelling. You wipe off the blood as best you can and hoist her backpack onto your shoulders. Leaning on you, she hops and hobbles her way home, grateful for such a kind friend.

A kind person is considerate, tenderhearted, and gentle. Kind people are soothing to be around, as they tend to be friendly, forgiving, and generous. A kind person shows sympathy for someone having a hard time, often bringing healing simply by listening. Kindness is a fruit of the Holy Spirit.

It's easier to be kind to our friends than to those who are strangers. It's most difficult to be kind to those we don't like. But true kindness is a choice, a trait produced in you by submitting to the work of the Holy Spirit after you become a believer. Be determined to sow seeds of kindness today!

WHAT'S A GIRL TO DO?

Which girl is showing the trait of kindness?

☐ Libby gets home from school first and eats the last jelly doughnut quickly before her brother notices it.

☐ Becky finds a little girl crying in the church rest-room and asks if she needs help finding her mom.

☐ Cassie notices that her grandma's flowers are dying. She feels sad that no one remembers to water them.

CONNECTING TO GOD

Dear Lord, I'm so grateful for the kindness you show me. Help me today to notice people who need extra kindness from me. Amen.

more to explore

Your kindness will reward you, but your cruelty will destroy you.

—Proverbs 11:17 (NLT)

FROM CRITICAL ...

"Do not judge others, and you will not be judged. For
you will be treated as you treat others."
—Matthew 7:1–2 (NLT)

Alexis was school shopping with her mom and little sister,
and each girl was buying a new fall jacket. Alexis chose a
jean jacket, but Myra (a chubby second grader) was having a more difficult time. She loved the red jacket with the
black dots and black trim, but she also liked the yellow
and black rain slicker. Alexis thought her sister looked fat
in both choices. She didn't want to be cruel so she said,
"Neither coat really looks good on you. Your round belly
really shows when you wear the red jacket, and your legs
look short when you wear the yellow one."

Myra's round face slowly crumpled. Tears welled up,
and she mumbled, "I don't want a new jacket, Mom. Let's
go home."

A critical person frequently finds fault with people. She
tends to make hurtful remarks—thinking she's just trying
to help. She finds many things to disapprove of, and her
opinions are often severe and unflattering. No one wants a
critical person for a friend or a sister!

People are critical for many reasons. Sometimes they
are copying a critical parent or older sibling. Sometimes a

critical person tries to make herself look better by finding fault with someone else. If you are critical often enough, it can become a hard habit to break. Instead, ask God to help you change into a person who looks for the good in others.

WHAT'S A GIRL TO DO?

Which girl is showing the trait of being critical?

- ☐ Mira notices her friend's new haircut and tells her, "I liked your hair better when it was longer."
- ☐ Cassie sees that her brother missed a small section when he mowed the yard, but she doesn't say anything to him about it.
- ☐ Becky's dad has made a new recipe for dinner. Becky politely eats a small portion even though she doesn't like it much.

CONNECTING TO GOD

Dear Lord, you have made an amazing world that is full of surprises and challenges. Help me to see the good in others even when they are different from me. Amen.

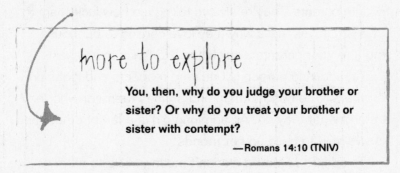

more to explore

You, then, why do you judge your brother or sister? Or why do you treat your brother or sister with contempt?

—Romans 14:10 (TNIV)

**Respect everyone and love your Christian brothers
and sisters.**

—1 Peter 2:17 (NLT)

Tomorrow night you are having friends over for a sleepover.
You already picked out the snacks, drinks, and music. You
really need to get to bed now, so your mom and dad offer
to rearrange the furniture to make room for all the sleeping
bags in the living room. The next morning, you see that your
mom and dad also decorated the living room, and the deco-
rations seem a little young—even babyish. You can see that
your parents are pleased and are waiting for your response.
You quickly search the room for something to praise and
say, "Thank you for your hard work. I love the colors of the
streamers." And then you add, "You know you're my friends'
favorite parents. They're always telling me how lucky I am to
have you guys. That's why they love coming to our house."
You give your parents a quick hug and thank them again.

An admiring person is one who respects and looks up
to others. She honors them and praises them for who they
are and what they do. An admiring girl is a fan of others and
knows how to build up her friends.

To admire someone doesn't mean you lie to them or
give false flattery. An admiring person genuinely notices
positive things about others. She is alert to opportunities to

remark on something special about that person or the job they've done. Believe it or not, some people go *years* without anyone admiring them. Don't let your family or friends starve for admiration. Notice good things about people, and speak up! Tell them!

WHAT'S A GIRL TO DO?

Which girls are showing the trait of admiring others?

☐ Libby's mom isn't sure if she likes the color she just painted the living room. Libby tells her, "I love the new color, Mom! You are so good at picking out colors."

☐ Rose sees that the school custodian has shoveled the front walk, and she is glad she won't get her shoes wet in the sloppy snow.

☐ Cassie goes to her little brother's open house. When she finds his clay pot in the art room, she says, "I love how you always choose such bright colors."

CONNECTING TO GOD

Dear Lord, I admire you so much for your love and mercy. I am grateful to have loving people in my life. Help me to be an admiring person to someone else today. Amen.

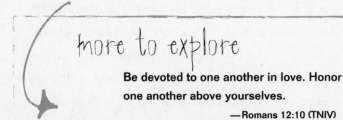

more to explore

Be devoted to one another in love. Honor one another above yourselves.

—Romans 12:10 (TNIV)

> A proud and haughty man—"Scoffer" is his name;
> he acts with arrogant pride.
>
> —Proverbs 21:24 (NKJV)

Kelsey started middle school this year, and she is very careful to wear the "right" clothes. She is highly pleased with her slender, athletic-looking appearance and long blonde hair. Her older sister in high school is more plump-ish. By nature, she is also quieter, preferring books to athletics. Kelsey doesn't allow for differences, however, and she looks down on her older sister. Frequently, Kelsey advises her sister to start a diet-and-exercise program or update her frumpy wardrobe. Kelsey feels superior and assumes that her older sister would prefer to look like Kelsey.

A girl who is haughty is disdainful of others, looking down on people from her "high-and-mighty" position. Stuck-up and snobbish, she is full of her own importance. She secretly believes that she is truly superior to others.

Being haughty and thinking you're better than others is a very unattractive trait. Few people want haughty friends. Snobbishness comes from being puffed up with pride, and the Bible says that God hates a prideful heart.

Take an honest look at yourself and ask, "Do I think I'm better than others in any way (for example, appearance, brains, or physical abilities)? How do I treat others when I have this attitude?" You might not like the answer, but give it some thought!

WHAT'S A GIRL TO DO?

Which girls are showing the trait of haughtiness?

- ☐ Kayla watches her friend making a pizza and says, "Here. I'll show you how to do it right."
- ☐ Becky is proud of her painting and thinks it is probably better than her friend's, but she also remembers that her friend is a much better runner than she is.
- ☐ Libby gets in the car next to her mom and says, "You're not wearing *that* old skirt to church, are you?"

CONNECTING TO GOD

Dear Lord, it's easy to compare my strengths to someone else's weak areas, but I don't want to do that. Help me not to think more highly of myself than I should. Amen.

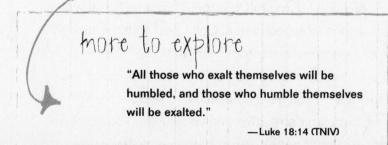

more to explore

"All those who exalt themselves will be humbled, and those who humble themselves will be exalted."

—Luke 18:14 (TNIV)

... TO HUMBLE

All of you, clothe yourselves with humility toward one another, because, "God opposes the proud but shows favor to the humble and oppressed."

—1 Peter 5:5 (TNIV)

On the first Thanksgiving after your dad remarried, pumpkin pie aroma drifts upstairs. You follow the smell into the kitchen where your stepmom is rushing around, obviously upset and overwhelmed. It looks like she's been up and cooking for hours. There are two pies on the stovetop, a turkey and a bowl of stuffing on the counter, and baking ingredients everywhere. "What's wrong?" you ask, wondering where your dad is. She sniffles and forces a smile. "Oh, nothing. I wanted this first Thanksgiving to be special, and look! I managed to burn the pies."

You can see that the pies *are* burned, but you say, "Don't feel bad. The stove's thermostat isn't quite right. My dad and I burn stuff in it too. They'll be fine if we just pile on the whipped cream. Can I help with the turkey?" Your new stepmom smiles with gratitude.

To be *humble* means "to be modest or meek—and teachable." You have a healthy and *realistic view* of yourself, both your strengths and your faults. You don't consider yourself better than someone else. (However, don't go around saying you're a "nothing." God doesn't make junk either.) A humble person knows that all people are "fearfully and wonderfully made" (Psalm 139:14 NKJV).

A girl who's humble makes a great friend and a great sister. Form the habit of mentally reminding yourself of other people's strengths. Then you won't be likely to think too highly of yourself. Remember, we're all equal, and God made each of us wonderful.

WHAT'S A GIRL TO DO?

Which girls are showing the trait of being humble?

- ☐ Kayla watches the new boy in art class sculpt a horse, then asks, "Can you show me how to do that?"
- ☐ Libby writes an essay for class and asks her friend to read it and give her constructive feedback.
- ☐ Mira is a very talented singer herself, but whenever someone else sings in church, she tells them, "I really enjoyed your song today."

CONNECTING TO GOD

Dear Lord, thank you for making us all special. Forgive me for the times when I've been snooty or snobbish. Amen.

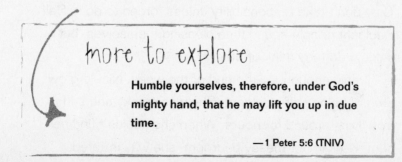

more to explore

Humble yourselves, therefore, under God's mighty hand, that he may lift you up in due time.

—1 Peter 5:6 (TNIV)

FROM SELF-INDULGENT ...

> You say, "I am allowed to do anything"—but, not
> everything is good for you. And even though "I am
> allowed to do anything," I must not become a slave to
> anything.
>
> —1 Corinthians 6:12 (NLT)

Nicole's grandma was staying with her for a week while her parents were on a trip. Nicole knew her grandma would never yell at her to set the table, clean her room, or fold the laundry. If Nicole left things unfinished long enough, Grandma would do the jobs herself. When Grandma visited, Nicole spent her evenings on the couch watching videos, ate a lot of junk food, and let her bedroom pile up with dirty clothes and wet towels.

People who are self-indulgent have habits that are excessive. They eat too much junk food and not enough healthy food. They lie around and let others do their work. They don't take responsibility unless forced to do it. Self-indulgent people spend time pleasing themselves, but seldom do they think of others.

Oddly enough, by the end of the week, Nicole grew tired of being self-indulgent. She was cranky and stiff from lying around for hours. When she couldn't find her homework in her messy bedroom, she was irritated.

Her stomach hurt from eating too much sugar. Taking care of her needs for food and rest *were* a good thing. Indulging herself too much, however, did more harm than good. Nicole finally realized that being moderate and self-controlled would leave her feeling better.

WHAT'S A GIRL TO DO?

Which girl is showing the trait of self-indulgence?

- ☐ After babysitting her neighbor, Rose is exhausted, so she takes a thirty-minute power nap before she studies for her history quiz.
- ☐ Libby goes for a forty-five-minute run before dinner. She is so hungry when she gets back, she eats an apple to hold her over until dinner.
- ☐ Cassie spends the evening watching a movie. When the movie is over, she notices she has about fifteen minutes until bedtime. She slips in another DVD.

CONNECTING TO GOD

Dear Lord, I am amazed at the way all the parts of the world work together in your hands. I want to take care of myself and treat others with respect. Help me do my part the way you want me to. Amen.

more to explore

Like a city whose walls are broken through is a person who lacks self-control.
—Proverbs 25:28 (TNIV)

... TO SELF-CONTROLLED

The fruit of the Spirit is ... self-control.
—Galatians 5:22–23 (TNIV)

You and your best friend are assigned a science report together. After school on Friday, you're meeting in the library to do your internet research. After school, you gather your materials on crossbreeding plants and head to the library. On the way, your friend stops you. "Wait!" she calls breathlessly. "Everybody's going to the mall for pizza and a movie. Wanna go?" You're tempted; anything sounds better on a Friday afternoon than the library. However, the project's due Monday, and you don't have internet access at home. "Sorry," you finally say, "I think I'll stay here and finish the research." Your friend frowns, and then surprises you by grinning. "You're right. We can always see the movie tomorrow."

A girl who is self-controlled is able to discipline herself. Self-control is needed for deciding what to eat, how to spend leisure time, and where to spend your money. Self-control helps you finish homework and chores, get adequate sleep and exercise, and choose the right words to speak. Being self-controlled means, with God's help, you are able to restrain—or stop—yourself from being irresponsible or excessive.

Self-control doesn't just happen to you by accident. You must be determined to develop this trait. Your own willpower won't take you very far, though. True and lasting self-control is possible only with the help of the Holy Spirit.

WHAT'S A GIRL TO DO?

Which girl is showing the trait of self-control?

☐ Becky has about two hours of homework to do today. She wants to get it done, but when her friend calls, she agrees to go to her friend's house.

☐ Cassie notices that they have four boxes of her favorite Girl Scout cookies, so she takes one to her bedroom and eats the whole box.

☐ Becky counts her allowance, sets aside her offering, deposits a little in her savings account, and puts the rest in her wallet.

CONNECTING TO GOD

Dear Lord, thank you for giving me the strength to do what is right, even when it is difficult. Amen.

more to explore

All athletes are disciplined in their training. They do it to win a prize that will fade away, but we do it for an eternal prize.

—1 Corinthians 9:25 (NLT)

FROM BLAMING . . .

"How dare you go on persecuting me, saying, 'It's his own fault'?"

—Job 19:28 (NLT)

Jasmine and her stepbrother attended the same middle school. On Monday morning, Jasmine was taking her geography project—a volcano model—to school. When climbing out of their minivan, she dropped the volcano. Her stepbrother, right behind her, accidentally stepped on it while backing out of the van. Jasmine screamed at him that he'd ruined her project. "It's your fault if I get a bad grade!" she yelled. She repeated her version of the incident all day to anyone who would listen—including the geography teacher. In her mind, it was crystal clear: her stepbrother was totally to blame for Jasmine's ruined school project.

A blaming type of girl is someone who accuses others. She pins the responsibility for some incident onto another person. It's always someone else's fault. A person who blames others often has difficulty seeing her own faults or weaknesses—even when she does the exact same things she blames others for! Rather than work on her problems, she blames others for her troubles.

If you tend to blame others, you'll find yourself with few friends. *And take note*: if you never honestly examine the part you play in the problem, things won't change. You'll be stuck with the same problems as you wait for someone else to fix things. Learn to pray for wisdom, then take responsibility for your part.

WHAT'S A GIRL TO DO?

Which girl is showing the trait of blaming?

- ☐ Mira gets soaked in a sudden downpour and regrets not bringing her rain poncho to the game.
- ☐ Libby forgets to shut her bedroom door to keep the dog out. She yells at the dog for chewing her slipper.
- ☐ Cassie eats three pieces of cake. Later she is sorry when she gets a bellyache.

CONNECTING TO GOD

Dear Lord, you are so forgiving of my many faults. Help me to be more like you. I'd like to see the good in others and take responsibility for my actions. Amen.

more to explore

You, then, why do you judge your brother or sister? Or why do you treat your brother or sister with contempt?

—Romans 14:10 (TNIV)

... TO RESPONSIBLE

We are each responsible for our own conduct.

—Galatians 6:5 (NLT)

You no longer want to attend youth group because it's boring. Kids gather in the back of the room and whisper among themselves; few respond to the leader's study questions. And the social events! Who comes up with those lame ideas? They obviously have no clue what kids your age like to do. Over Sunday dinner, you tell your parents that you're not interested in belonging to youth group. After listing your reasons, you expect them to agree with you. Instead, your dad says, "You've described the situation well. How can you be part of the solution?"

A girl who is responsible is dependable and honest. She's mature in how she responds to people and situations. Rather than cast blame, a responsible person will examine herself first. "What is my part in this problem?" she'll ask. "How did I contribute to it? What can I do to solve the problem?"

Your dad's question makes you rethink the youth group. Being responsible for your own actions means, in this case, admitting you're guilty of everything you complained about. You gossip with friends instead of responding to the leader's questions. When they chose the book to study, you didn't offer any suggestions. A planning committee was formed to arrange the social activities—but you refused to join. You decide now to be responsible and do your part toward making the youth group an active—and fun—group of believers.

WHAT'S A GIRL TO DO?

Which girls are showing the trait of being responsible?

- ☐ Becky asks her English teacher if the class may perform a play for the whole school. Becky volunteers to talk to the principal and design a poster to hang up at school.
- ☐ Kayla receives a poor science grade mainly because she didn't turn in all of her homework assignments. She complains that the teacher isn't fair.
- ☐ Rose sets a running goal for herself and keeps track of her exercise times on a calendar. After she has a routine, she invites her friends to join her a couple of days a week.

CONNECTING TO GOD

Dear Lord, you continue to love me even when I let you down. Thank you for your faith in me. Help me to be responsible for my own actions. Amen.

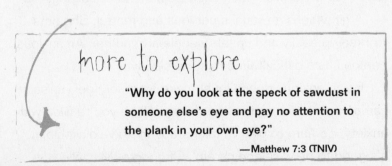

more to explore

"Why do you look at the speck of sawdust in someone else's eye and pay no attention to the plank in your own eye?"

—Matthew 7:3 (TNIV)

FROM ANXIOUS . . .

Do not be anxious about anything, but in every situation, by prayer and petition, with thanksgiving, present your requests to God.

—Philippians 4:6 (TNIV)

Michelle took her little sister, Molly, shopping for their dad's birthday gift. It didn't take long for little Molly to get bored. Michelle looked at ties and smelled aftershave, finally choosing a book. Next were the birthday cards. When Michelle finally selected a funny card and turned around to show it to Molly, her little sister wasn't there. Michelle dashed to the end of the aisle and glanced both ways. No Molly. *She's been kidnapped!* Michelle thought. She ran to the checker in tears. "My sister's missing!" Her voice was loud and shrill. "Help me! It's an emergency! Call the police!" When Molly heard her sister's voice, she quickly ran to her sister from the next aisle and started crying.

A girl who is anxious is nervous and fearful. She gets worked up easily and upsets people around her. An anxious person has a difficult time thinking clearly.

Being anxious doesn't just make a person feel worse; it can actually make a situation worse. When you're filled with anxiety, it's hard to plan or take steps to solve a problem. It's good to be wise and careful. Of course, Michelle was concerned about her little sister and got help to find her. But an anxious girl makes circumstances worse by becoming hysterical. Instead, she needs to give her anxious thoughts and feelings to God—and receive his peace in return. Trading anxiety for peace is a great arrangement!

WHAT'S A GIRL TO DO?

Which girl is showing the trait of being anxious?

- ☐ While babysitting, Mira locks all the doors after she puts the kids to bed and then settles down to do her homework.
- ☐ Cassie listens to weather reports around the country on TV. In the morning, she doesn't want to go to school because she is afraid of severe weather.
- ☐ Kayla's family moves to a new neighborhood. Kayla is eager to go to the neighborhood swimming pool, hoping to meet some girls her age.

CONNECTING TO GOD

Dear Lord, thank you for the peace you bring me when I pray. Help me remember to go to you when I feel anxious. Amen.

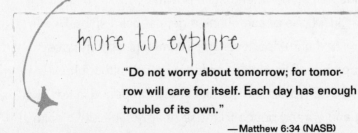

more to explore

"Do not worry about tomorrow; for tomorrow will care for itself. Each day has enough trouble of its own."

—Matthew 6:34 (NASB)

... to PEACEFUL

You will keep in perfect peace all who trust in you, all whose thoughts are fixed on you!

—Isaiah 26:3 (NLT)

You're playing softball in the vacant lot next to your house one hot Saturday afternoon. You bat the ball hard, sending the softball in a straight line to your best friend. The ball slips between her hands and hits her in the eye, knocking her flat. Dizzy and head pounding, she lies there as you and your sister lean over her. Your wide-eyed sister Lily screams for your mom. Your best friend starts to cry. You can see she is getting worried, so you take a deep breath, pray for God's healing and strength, and pat her arm. You calmly tell your sister to go get your dad. After Lily runs off, you tell your friend, "I'm sorry. Just relax and close your eyes. My dad will be here in a minute." Your peaceful attitude helps your friend calm down.

A girl who is peaceful has a gentle, calm spirit. She is serene and unruffled, even in circumstances that upset other people. She isn't necessarily silent, although she can be. The words she speaks show the peace in her own heart and spread peace to those nearby. She stays calm in the middle of a storm.

Focusing on God's strength and care will keep us calm. And when we're calm, we think and feel better. So do the people around us. Let God's peace fill you at all times.

WHAT'S A GIRL TO DO?

Which girls are showing the trait of being peaceful?

- ☐ Cassie is a dollar short in the checkout line at the grocery store, so she puts the candy bar back.
- ☐ Libby can't answer the first two questions on the test, so she slams her pencil down on the desk.
- ☐ Becky hears her parents arguing, and she prays for God to help them find a solution to their problem.

CONNECTING TO GOD

Dear Lord, thank you for giving me your peace. Help me to create peaceful relationships with others too. Amen.

more to explore

The peace of God, which transcends all understanding, will guard your hearts and your minds in Christ Jesus.
—Philippians 4:7 (TNIV)

FROM UNDEPENDABLE ...

"My brothers are as undependable as intermittent streams."

—Job 6:15 (TNIV)

Amber found the note from her dad while making her after-school snack. Her older sister's band concert was that night. Her dad was reminding Amber to have supper ready for the family. They'd need to leave almost immediately for the concert. Amber ate her snack and watched a TV show, then called her friend Callie about something weird that had happened on the way home. When Amber's dad drove in the driveway, Amber remembered supper—which was still waiting to be fixed. That night they all ate cold cereal for supper because there wasn't time to cook. Amber's mom and dad were clearly irritated, but Amber just rolled her eyes. It wasn't her fault she was busy after school.

An undependable girl tends to be irresponsible or inconsistent about keeping promises. Undependable people make difficult friends because you can't count on them to keep their word.

Amber wasn't too busy after school to fix supper; she was undependable. Her own wishes and interests meant more to her than her dad's request. Thinking of

72

self-interests first is generally the root cause of being undependable. Make sure your responsibilities to others come before your own fun if you want to be reliable. You'll feel better about yourself, and your friends and family will be grateful that they can depend on your word.

WHAT'S A GIRL TO DO?

Which girls seem undependable?

- ☐ Mira is too tired to show up for skit practice at youth group, so she takes a nap instead.
- ☐ Kayla promises to keep her friend's secret about moving, so she tells only one other girl, who promises not to tell.
- ☐ Libby says she will babysit for the neighbors on Saturday night, so she turns down an invitation to the movies that night with her best friend.

CONNECTING TO GOD

Dear Lord, thank you that I can always count on you and your Word. Help me also to be dependable in all I say and do. Amen.

more to explore

Their hearts were not loyal to him, they were not faithful to his covenant.
—Psalm 78:37 (TNIV)

... to RELIABLE

My dear brothers and sisters, stand firm.
Let nothing move you.

—1 Corinthians 15:58 (TNIV)

You're in charge of your younger stepbrother after school.
On many afternoons, you bike with him to a park three
blocks away so he can have fun on the playground equipment. One day, your friends from school show up, asking
if you want to get ice cream with them. They invite you to
bring your little brother along. You're not allowed to go anywhere with friends while babysitting, but probably no one
would ever know. No doubt your stepbrother would keep
quiet if he were promised ice cream. And yet, your mom
and stepdad depend on you to keep a close eye on your
brother. That's hard to do when with your friends. You feel
disappointed, but you say no to the ice cream.

A reliable girl is trustworthy and responsible. She is
faithful to keep her promises. A reliable person can be
depended on, no matter what temptations and distractions
come along. Being reliable isn't always easy, but God will
give you the strength and desire if you ask him.

Being reliable in the little things—chores, homework,
walking the dog, giving at church—will encourage your

parents and teachers to give you more privileges. As you grow, they'll be able to trust you for bigger things, like one day driving a car. Employers also search for dependable workers and will be glad to give you a job. Choose today to work on the trait of being reliable. There are many rewards!

WHAT'S A GIRL TO DO?

Which girl seems reliable?

- ◯ While the neighbors are on vacation, Rose promises to walk their dog, but when it rains, she decides to skip it and give the dog a rest.
- ◯ On the morning of a school presentation on the Civil War, Becky hasn't prepared her part so she copies some information off the Internet to read.
- ◯ Kayla races uptown on her bike and arrives a few minutes early for her dental appointment.

CONNECTING TO GOD

Dear Lord, help me to be a girl people can count on. Thank you for being my rock. Amen.

more to explore

An unreliable messenger stumbles into trouble, but a reliable messenger brings healing.

—Proverbs 13:17 (NLT)

FROM RUDE . . .

The heart of the righteous weighs its answers, but the mouth of the wicked gushes evil.

—Proverbs 15:28

Kyla's stepdad was, in her opinion, way too nosy about her friends, her activities, and her schoolwork. She didn't like him asking questions, so she was rude to him whenever she thought he was being nosy. If he questioned where she was going, she said, "Out." When he quizzed her about who was on the phone, she said, "A friend." If he asked if she had her homework done when she was watching TV, she stared at him without answering. Surely he'd get the point soon and leave her alone.

A person who is rude shows bad manners. She isn't courteous or understanding. You can be rude with your words by spouting insults or snapping at people. Actions can also be discourteous, as when making impatient or unfriendly gestures.

Sometimes rude people are taking out their anger on others. Or they believe they're more important than others. Sometimes rude people are impatient, demanding that the world revolve around them. Regardless of the reason behind it, followers of Jesus have no business being rude to others.

Instead, unbelievers should recognize that we're his children because of the love we show others. One way to do that is with our words. Make a decision to be polite and show respect and love to others.

WHAT'S A GIRL TO DO?

Which girls are showing the trait of rudeness?

- ◯ Because she can see a woman standing with her tray scanning the room for an empty table, Cassie slips into the last empty booth in the fast-food restaurant while her friends wait in line to order.
- ◯ The librarian asks Becky to log off the Internet so someone else can use the computer. She says "Sure," even though she wishes she could keep emailing.
- ◯ Rose laughs at her little sister when she does an awkward cartwheel across the lawn.

CONNECTING TO GOD

Dear Lord, forgive me for the times I've been rude to others. I want to show your love by being kind and polite in all my words and actions. Amen.

more to explore

Set a guard over my mouth, O LORD; keep watch over the door of my lips.

—Psalm 141:3

... TO POLITE

I said, "I will watch my ways and keep my tongue
from sin."

—Psalm 39:1 (TNIV)

One warm spring afternoon, you're strolling with two friends
across the front lawn of your school. One of your friends
snickers at the custodian watering petunias around the
base of each maple tree. She points to the custodian's
baggy coveralls and gardening boots and makes a joke
about "hillbillies." The custodian waters the last plant, turns,
and walks in your direction. He nods to several students.
When he gets near your group, your friend mimics his walk.
Ignoring your friend, you catch the custodian's eye and say,
"Thanks for making the school grounds look beautiful." The
custodian's grin makes your day.

A polite girl is caring and gracious, thoughtful and lady-
like. A polite person considers the other person's feelings when deciding how to speak or act. Being polite is
one excellent way to show God's love to others at home,
school, and in the community.

Sometimes people think it's cool to be rude—and old-
fashioned to be polite. Rude movie stars and professional
athletes are often seen as heroes. Not according to God's
Word! How you use your tongue—to bring pain to others

or to lift their spirits—reveals a lot about the inner condition of your heart. Words are powerful; they can be used as weapons or instruments of healing. Make it a practice to be polite (kind and considerate) to everyone—parents, teachers, siblings, friends, and strangers. Pray for the love of God to be spread from your heart to the world.

WHAT'S A GIRL TO DO?

Which girls are showing the trait of politeness?

☐ When Kayla's way into the theater is blocked by a group of laughing girls, she says, "Excuse me, can I get past you?"

☐ Libby answers the phone and says, "What do you want?"

☐ Rose bumps into a toddler, stoops down to her eye level, and says, "I'm sorry. Are you okay?"

CONNECTING TO GOD

Dear Lord, thank you for teaching us the importance of the words we say. Help me to be polite and share your love with others. Amen.

more to explore

Those who consider themselves religious and yet do not keep a tight rein on their tongues deceive themselves, and their religion is worthless.

—James 1:26 (TNIV)

devotion 37

**My wound is severe, and my grief is great. My sick-
ness is incurable, but I must bear it.**

—Jeremiah 10:19 (NLT)

Brianna's new baby brother was born with three holes in
his heart. One was dangerously large and not expected
to close on its own. Brianna didn't understand everything
she overheard of her parents' whispered conversations,
but she knew the situation was desperate. Little Joshua
needed two open-heart surgeries. His weakened condition
and tiny size were two strikes against him. Brianna saw the
desperation on her parents' faces and understood. She felt
overwhelmed and totally helpless herself.

Someone who is desperate is filled with despair and
feels her situation is beyond help and hope. The situation
she faces feels extremely critical, maybe even calling for
drastic action. A desperate person sometimes says she
is "at the end of her rope." When a person doesn't know
Jesus as her Savior, she probably won't see God as a true
source of help. That's very scary and can certainly leave
someone feeling desperate.

God doesn't ever want to leave us desperate. There
are no circumstances too big for God to help, control,

or change. Often, it is a desperate situation that turns a person to God, crying out for salvation and help. We seem to know instinctively that only God can make a difference in our situation. Only God can turn our desperation to hope.

WHAT'S A GIRL TO DO?

Which girls are showing the trait of desperation?

- ☐ When Becky falls off her bike and breaks her collarbone, she lies on the sidewalk, praying for help and waiting for it to come.
- ☐ Maddie watches her dad pack his suitcase to leave the family, and she wishes she were dead.
- ☐ Ellie accidentally rips a valuable stamp in her sister's stamp collection. She is afraid to tell her sister so she hides the stamp collection in a place she thinks her sister will never find it.

CONNECTING TO GOD

Dear Lord, I'm so grateful that you're always there for me, especially when something is difficult to face! Help me share your love with others who might be in a desperate situation. Amen.

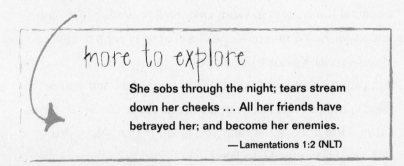

more to explore

She sobs through the night; tears stream down her cheeks ... All her friends have betrayed her; and become her enemies.
—Lamentations 1:2 (NLT)

... TO HOPEFUL

Be of good courage, and He shall strengthen your heart, all you who hope in the LORD.

—Psalm 31:24 (NKJV)

You love playing the flute, and you love band. When your teacher is injured in a car accident and replaced by another music instructor, you miss the former teacher very much. The new teacher frowns a lot, giving the impression that he doesn't like kids or teaching band. Although your friends don't like him, you're hopeful that he'll loosen up. Maybe he's not used to kids your age. (You heard he used to teach college band.) You are optimistic that once he gets familiar with the students and routine, band will be fun again.

A hopeful person is optimistic, expecting good things to happen to her. She's easily encouraged, seeing events or people as promising and favorable. A believer has hope because her trust is in God, who is all-powerful, all-loving, and all-wise. When someone like that is in control of your life, it's much easier to be hopeful!

When you expect good things to happen and you're filled with faith and hope, good things do occur much more often. God honors the faith you place in him. Also, you behave differently when filled with hope. With the new band teacher, you're friendly and encouraging. Smiling, you say you're glad he's there. You show enthusiasm about the music he wants the band to learn. Before long, the new teacher is more relaxed and more fun. God has undoubtedly worked on his heart and mind. Quite possibly he's used your friendly hopefulness to help bring about change.

WHAT'S A GIRL TO DO?

Which girls are showing the trait of hopefulness?

- ☐ Cassie makes party favors for all the people she invited to her party, expecting most of them to show up.
- ☐ Becky signs up for softball tryouts, confident that she'll make the team.
- ☐ Kayla doesn't answer the phone, fearful that it's her dad saying he's not coming to her concert after all.

CONNECTING TO GOD

Dear Lord, thank you for being my hope when I have none. Help me to encourage others too. Amen.

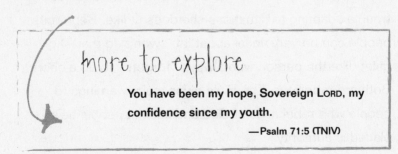

more to explore

You have been my hope, Sovereign LORD, my confidence since my youth.
—Psalm 71:5 (TNIV)

FROM REBELLIOUS...

"Rebellion is as sinful as witchcraft, and stubbornness as bad as worshiping idols."

—1 Samuel 15:23 (NLT)

Stephanie lived in a cold climate. She loved summer and hated winter. Her mom and dad repeatedly had to remind her to wear her mittens, hat, and winter coat. Irritated, Stephanie thought it should be up to her whether she wore winter clothes—and she tried to avoid them. Besides, it wasn't "cool" to wear a lot of heavy clothes. On a cold morning, Stephanie's mom wrapped a scarf around her neck and tried to hand her a hat and mittens as she walked out the door. Stephanie pretended not to see and stomped away.

A rebellious person resists being told what to do by anyone and may show a real stubborn streak. She has trouble adapting to situations she doesn't like. Rebellious people can be very vocal about it ("I won't do that!") or quiet (like the person who always "forgets" to do a chore). Both are rebellious. The Bible gives many warnings to people who rebel against God and against people he's placed in authority.

The problem of rebellion may stem from a self-centered heart. The rebellious person wants her own way—*period.*

Rebellion can also come from anger or fear of not being accepted. If rebellion is a problem for you, ask God to help you understand *why* you struggle with this. Then ask him for a discerning spirit to know when to obey and when to stand up against injustice.

WHAT'S A GIRL TO DO?

Which girl is showing the trait of rebelliousness?

- ☐ Rose hurries home to babysit her little brother after school, even though she doesn't want to.
- ☐ Caroline glances both ways and then drops her candy bar wrapper on the ground.
- ☐ Libby ignores her whispering friends and quietly studies her math problems.

CONNECTING TO GOD

Dear Lord, help me understand when it is time to stand up for what is right and when it is time to be obedient. You are my guide. Create in me an open and loving heart. Amen.

more to explore

"If you are willing and obedient, you will eat the best from the land; but if you resist and rebel, you will be devoured by the sword."

—Isaiah 1:19–20 (TNIV)

... TO OBEDIENT

**"Blessed rather are those who hear the word of God
and obey it."**

—Luke 11:28 (TNIV)

You're spending the weekend with your grandparents while
your mom is on a business trip. On Saturday afternoon
you're engrossed in your favorite action-filled DVD. Deli-
cious smells of fried chicken waft from the kitchen. The
movie's half over when Grandma calls to you from the
dining room: "I need you to set the table for supper now."
Rats! You wish you could finish the movie—it's at the most
exciting part. But you push Stop on the remote control,
wipe the scowl off your face, and go set the table anyway.

An obedient girl is one who yields to authority. She
does what she is asked by parents, teachers, grandparents, government officials, and others whom God has
placed in authority over her. An obedient person is dutiful
and conforms to the rules and expectations of those over
her. (*Important*: she also does it with a good attitude—no
arguments or protests.)

An obedient Christian is one who does what God commands in the Bible. There are many rewards for the believer
who submits to God's Word. Obedient followers can have
confidence that when they go to God about their needs,

he'll answer their prayers (1 John 3:21–22). The path of obedience is the path of great blessing and freedom.

WHAT'S A GIRL TO DO?

Which girl is showing the trait of obedience?

- ☐ Libby leaves the shopping cart next to the car in the parking lot instead of putting it in the rack marked "Place carts here."
- ☐ Mira leaves her cell phone on in the theater, despite the request to turn it off, because she is expecting a call from her boyfriend.
- ☐ Kayla runs three extra laps when the coach orders her to, even though she thinks it's unfair.

CONNECTING TO GOD

Dear Lord, being obedient is so hard sometimes! Forgive me for my disobedience—and for the times I've obeyed, but with a rotten attitude. Help me to obey with joy. Amen.

more to explore

Don't you know that when you offer yourselves to someone as obedient slaves, you are slaves of the one you obey— whether you are slaves to sin, which leads to death, or to obedience, which leads to righteousness?

—Romans 6:16 (TNIV)

FROM SARCASTIC . . .

Your tongue plots destruction; it is like a sharpened razor.

—Psalm 52:2 (TNIV)

Emily and her friend were sitting on their bikes in the driveway when her older brother—all dressed up in his best shirt and pants—dashed out of the house. "Move it," he called, jumping into his old car.

Emily planted one hand on her jutting hip and rolled her eyes. "*Oooooh!* Lover Boy has a hot date," she whispered to her friend. Raising her voice, she said to her brother, "Don't you look cool. Your handsomeness is making us dizzy. And your car is sure to impress any girl with its beautiful rust."

Her brother yelled back, "Thanks for the kind words. I hope the kennel lets you off your leash soon."

A sarcastic person mocks or baits others in a biting kind of way. It is the opposite of what the Bible tells us to do, which is to "[speak] the truth in love" (Ephesians 4:15).

Sometimes people are sarcastic accidentally when they intend to be cute or funny. Be aware of how your words sound to others. There's a big difference between a humorous comment and a biting remark. Sarcastic people may take their anger out on someone by using cutting words. They may put someone down to make themselves appear more important. It doesn't work that way. They only come out looking mean and nasty. The next time a sarcastic comment almost escapes your lips, bite it back, swallow it, and let it die. It can't benefit anyone.

WHAT'S A GIRL TO DO?

Which girls are showing the trait of sarcasm?

- ☐ After Kayla is asked to move faster in the cafeteria line, she says, "Sorry to delay your fine-dining experience."
- ☐ Ellie notices a new girl in her gym class, rolls her eyes, and mumbles, "Nice shorts."
- ☐ Libby touches her sister's bare arm and says, "Ever hear of lotion?"

CONNECTING TO GOD

Dear Lord, you are too gracious to ever use sarcasm. Help me to control my tongue and keep from hurting others. Amen.

more to explore

Let no foul or polluting language, nor evil word nor unwholesome or worthless talk [ever] come out of your mouth.

—Ephesians 4:29 (AMP)

> We have all had parents who disciplined us and we
> respected them for it.
>
> —Hebrews 12:9 (TNIV)

You grab your towel to head out the door on Saturday
morning, ready for a day at the pool with your best friend.
Your mom asks if your room is clean. "It's good enough,"
you say, impatient to leave. "Let's go check," Mom says.
She opens your bedroom door. Her lips are pursed as
she notices your dirty clothes shoved halfway under the
bed and your messy pile of school papers. She turns to
you and says, "You might want to call Hannah. Looks like
you'll be cleaning for a while yet." You hang your head for
a moment, biting back an angry remark. "Okay, I'll call her,"
you say, determined to clean the room in record time.

Someone who is respectful is polite and well-mannered.
Speaking respectfully involves giving honor to someone or
holding them in high regard. A respectful girl is courteous
in her thoughts, words, and actions. She treats people—of
all ages and all backgrounds—in the same way Jesus
treated people.

We should respect everyone God has placed in authority over us. In the home, that's usually our parents or our

grandparents. At school we have teachers and coaches. At church there are the pastor and youth leader. In the mall, at theaters, and in public places, there are employees in charge. We also need to show respect to our peers—our equals—and those with less power (like younger brothers and sisters, the handicapped, and the elderly). *Everyone* deserves your respect.

WHAT'S A GIRL TO DO?

Which girl is showing the trait of respectfulness?

- ☐ When Mira's little brother asks her to play a game, without even looking his way she says, "Bug off."
- ☐ Becky takes a phone call for her brother and says, "He's not here, but he'll be back at four if you want to call then."
- ☐ When the soccer coach sends Lydia to the sidelines, she says, "I don't want to sit out."

CONNECTING TO GOD

Dear Lord, forgive me for all the times I have been disrespectful to people. Help me treat others as you treat me—with respect. Amen.

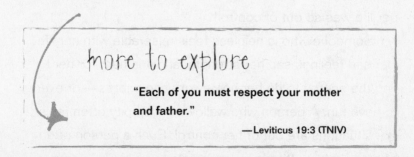

more to explore

"Each of you must respect your mother and father."

—Leviticus 19:3 (TNIV)

FROM HELPLESS ...

> **My spirit is overwhelmed within me; my heart within me is distressed.**
>
> —Psalm 143:4 (NKJV)

Liz studied her pile of unfinished homework. It just seemed like too much to do. She put her head down and cried. While she was sitting there, she remembered how her friends had ignored her that afternoon. Didn't they like her anymore? She felt miserable. And what about soccer practice last night? She just couldn't seem to get control of the ball. Did the team all talk behind her back about how bad she was? Maybe she should quit. Liz sat up and looked at her homework again. She just didn't know where to start. Her brother never had this much homework. It wasn't fair! "Why *me*, God?" she asked frequently. Liz felt very sorry for herself and spent many hours crying. It wasn't *her* fault her life was so out of control!

Someone who is helpless feels miserable with her life. Her sad feelings sap her strength, and it is hard for her to find the energy to do her homework and chores—or even to have fun. A person who wallows in self-pity often feels like situations are out of her control. Such a person often has a negative attitude or low spirits.

When we feel helpless to change our circumstances, it is time to turn to God—who *can* help and wants to help. We can then discover that God protects us from trouble and surrounds us with "songs of victory" (Psalm 32:7 NLT)!

WHAT'S A GIRL TO DO?

Which girl is showing the trait of helplessness?

- ☐ When Becky finds out that her dad lost his job, she asks, "How can I help?"
- ☐ When Rose receives a bad grade on her reading test, she goes to bed and cries herself to sleep.
- ☐ When Cassie's bike is stolen, she asks to borrow her brother's bike until she finds hers.

CONNECTING TO GOD

Dear Lord, thank you for being my rock when I feel down. Help me remember that tough times happen to everyone, and that I can handle my problems with your help. Amen.

more to explore

My days vanish like smoke; my bones burn like glowing embers. My heart is blighted and withered like grass; I forget to eat my food.

—Psalm 102:3–4 (TNIV)

We are more than conquerors and gain a surpassing victory through Him Who loved us.
—Romans 8:37 (AMP)

You and your best friend have leading parts in the youth-group skit for the Sunday night service. You're speaking, and your friend is singing. Since you will perform together onstage, you're confident it will go okay. However, just before leaving home Sunday night, your friend calls. She's running a fever, and her mom won't let her perform in the skit. She says the youth director wants you to both speak *and* sing, since you know her song. You panic, finding it hard to breathe. The idea of "winging it" without a rehearsal makes you dizzy with fear. You tell your parents, and they immediately pray with you, asking God to work through you and give you strength to perform both parts. Later, you perform both parts well, amazed at how well the skit goes.

When a person feels powerful, she feels energetic and in control, capable of handling life's big problems and every-day concerns. A follower of Jesus knows that she has no power of her own. Her power to overcome life's challenges comes from being controlled by the Holy Spirit.

Many days we face challenges—big and small—that require power beyond our own to do a good job.

When relying on ourselves, we may be nervous and only partly effective. When we count on the Holy Spirit's power, we can relax and let him be in charge. Nothing is too big to handle together!

WHAT'S A GIRL TO DO?

Which girls are showing the trait of being powerful?

- ⬭ Cassie's puppy runs outside and down the street. Cassie prays for wisdom and help before starting after him.
- ⬭ Kayla lies in the emergency room, waiting to have her hand stitched up. She trusts that the doctor will be there soon and that God will help her stand the pain.
- ⬭ Libby set a jump-rope goal for herself, but she keeps making mistakes. After several tries, she throws down the rope, sure that she'll never reach her goal.

CONNECTING TO GOD

Dear Lord, help me turn to you when I'm facing hard things. Thank you for always being there for me! Amen.

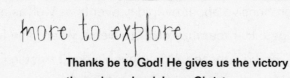

more to explore

Thanks be to God! He gives us the victory through our Lord Jesus Christ.

—1 Corinthians 15:57 (TNIV)

devotion 15

Fearing people is a dangerous trap, but trusting the
LORD means safety.

—Proverbs 29:25 (NLT)

Jessica babysat often and usually loved it, but tonight a
storm was brewing. The trees outside the Thompson house
bent so much in the wind that the longer branches tapped
the windows. Jessica knew the creaking and tapping were
caused by the storm. Yet the noise sounded to her exactly
like someone trying to break in. After doing all the necessary things—flipping on the outside yard lights and double-
checking that doors and windows are locked—Jessica
finally remembered to pray. Only then did her heart stop
racing. She could finally settle down and read her book until
Mr. and Mrs. Thompson got home.

A person who is fearful is easily frightened, sometimes
unreasonably. She may dread many things in life, feeling apprehensive about everyday events as well as major
challenges. Her fear may grow to alarm, where she feels
panicky and distressed. When people don't trust in God for
the help they need, they often live fearful lives.

It's normal to feel fear in many situations, especially
when trying something new or facing a sudden loss.

Fear can grow and take over our lives if we don't ask God to take it from us. When fear attacks, let it remind you that you're not alone. God's presence can dispel the fear. Pray, and pray often, during such times. The Lord can guide you to replace your fears with his courage.

WHAT'S A GIRL TO DO?

Which girls are showing the trait of fearfulness?

- ☐ While waiting for the science tests to be passed out, Rose squeezes her pencil so hard it snaps in two.
- ☐ When Mira opens her mouth to begin her oral report, her mind goes blank, and no words come out.
- ☐ When Becky meets a big dog on her walk, she calmly says a prayer and crosses to the other side of the street.

CONNECTING TO GOD

Dear Lord, thank you for your calming influence in my life. I'm glad I can ask you for help when I need it. Amen.

more to explore

God has not given us a spirit of fear, but of power and of love and of a sound mind.
—2 Timothy 1:7 (NKJV)

... TO BRAVE

> **"Be strong and courageous. Do not be afraid or terri-
> fied because of them, for the LORD your God goes with
> you; he will never leave you nor forsake you."**
> —Deuteronomy 31:6 (TNIV)

You ride the school bus every morning and afternoon for
an hour. You used to enjoy the time alone to read. Then the
new boy moved in and was assigned the seat behind you.
Now your nerves are constantly on edge, waiting for him to
yank your hair or poke you with a pencil or twist your arm.
The bus driver is never looking when the incidents occur.
The bully has threatened you with worse treatment if you
tell anyone. Lately your stomach hurts during the last hour
of school as you anticipate the ride home.

To be *brave* means "to show courage, or to be bold,
even when feeling attacked by fear." A brave person may
be called gutsy or daring. A follower of Jesus can be brave
because she knows that God will guide her and help her
meet her needs. It's much easier to be brave when you
remember that the God of the universe is on your side!

After praying about the bully, you wait for God to show
you what to do. You firmly tell the bully that you do not like
what he is doing and hope he will now leave you alone, but
instead he gets worse. One day he grabs your hat and hits

your head. This time the driver is watching and stops the bus. The bully is moved to an empty seat directly behind the driver for the rest of the school year. You breathe a sigh of relief and murmur, "Oh, thank you, Lord!"

WHAT'S A GIRL TO DO?

Which girls are showing the trait of bravery?

- ☐ Cassie throws away an invitation to a pool party, because she's afraid that her friends will discover she can't swim.
- ☐ Becky hears her mom crying in her bedroom and, despite her nervousness, knocks on the door to find out what is wrong.
- ☐ Kayla ignores her pounding heart, steps up to the mike, and auditions for the play.

CONNECTING TO GOD

Dear Lord, I can't be brave on my own. Thank you for giving me your courage! Amen.

more to explore

Wait for the LORD; be strong and let your heart take courage; yes, wait for the LORD.
—Psalm 27:14 (NASB)

FROM ARGUMENTATIVE ...

**Must I forever see these evil deeds? ... I am sur-
rounded by people who love to argue and fight.**
—Habakkuk 1:3 (NLT)

Madison shared a room with her stepsister, Leah. Leah
liked it quiet, but Madison liked to listen to music while she
studied. Leah dropped into bed at nine o'clock and wanted
the lights out by then. Madison, a night owl, wanted to
have the freedom to make noise till at least eleven. Whenever Leah asked her to turn off the music or turn off some
lights, Madison argued with her. "You can stay up later than
that. And you're going to have to get used to some noise,"
she added, turning up the volume. "Do you plan to live in a
soundproof, padded cell all your life?"

Argumentative people enjoy fighting. They have very
strong opinions and can find something to argue about on
most issues. They have a difficult time seeing the effect of
their actions on other people. The Bible warns us to avoid
people like this (Proverbs 22:10) and not to be argumentative ourselves (Proverbs 17:14).

Madison may have been angry about having to share
her room with her new stepsister. Sharing a room isn't
easy. But her arguing isn't a constructive way to deal with

her problems. It's not fair to others to pick fights and stir things up. Instead, she should deal directly with what's bothering her, come up with a compromise—and then live in peace.

WHAT'S A GIRL TO DO?

Which girl is showing the trait of being argumentative?

- ☐ Mira is told to take an umbrella because rain is forecast in the afternoon, and she says, "Thanks for telling me."
- ☐ Cassie's dad tells her to turn off the TV and go to bed; disappointed, she sighs and decides to watch the rest of the DVD the next night.
- ☐ Becky's mom tells her to feed the cat, and Becky says, "Why should I? It's not just my cat."

CONNECTING TO GOD

Dear Lord, teach me to find peace and understanding. Forgive me for not seeing another person's point of view. Thanks for loving me even when I am argumentative. Amen.

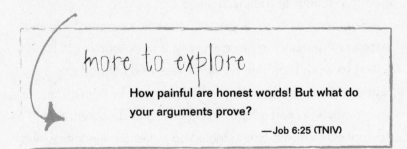

more to explore

How painful are honest words! But what do your arguments prove?

—Job 6:25 (TNIV)

"This matter is in your hands. We will support you, so take courage and do it."

—Ezra 10:4

You and your friends have plans Friday after school to go shoe shopping and then out for a pizza. You've looked forward to this all week. During last period on Friday, your art teacher calls you to her desk. She asks if you can possibly stay after school for an hour or so. She needs help putting out projects for the art festival being held in the cafeteria the following morning. "The teacher who was supposed to help me got called home on an emergency," she explains. You hesitate, then say, "Sure. I can stay and help." You tell your friends you're skipping the shopping trip, but you'll meet them later at the pizza place.

Someone who is cooperative makes a wonderful friend! Instead of demanding her own way, a cooperative girl is willing to work together, compromise, and help others. Rather than argue about minor differences of opinion, a cooperative person adapts to others. She demonstrates several fruits of the Spirit, including patience, kindness, and gentleness.

We all need help sometimes. It's such a joy to find someone who is willing to cooperate and help out. Being cooperative requires that you be *others*-centered instead of *self*-centered, placing others' interests above your own. "Let each of you look out not only for his own interests, but also for the interests of others" (Philippians 2:4 NKJV).

WHAT'S A GIRL TO DO?

Which girls are showing the trait of being cooperative?

- ☐ On Sunday morning, Libby doesn't feel like going to church, and she takes so long getting showered and dressed that her family is late to arrive.
- ☐ Kayla prefers to see a science-fiction movie on Saturday afternoon, but it's her brother's turn to choose, so she watches the animated feature he picks.
- ☐ Rose stands up on the full bus and offers her seat to a young woman carrying a baby.

CONNECTING TO GOD

Dear Lord, I admit that sometimes I just want my own way. Help me to think of others more. Amen.

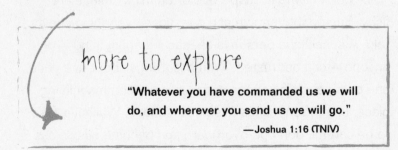

more to explore

"Whatever you have commanded us we will do, and wherever you send us we will go."
—Joshua 1:16 (TNIV)

FROM SUSPICIOUS ...

"Stop pointing your finger and spreading vicious rumors!"

—Isaiah 58:9 (NLT)

One Saturday morning while mowing the lawn, Haley notices the girl across the street. She is a year older than Haley and shy. She's had a crush on Haley's older brother for months. This morning the girl is limping as she emerges from the house and climbs into their family car. She glances over and waves, but Haley doesn't wave back. *Talk about a drama queen*, Haley thinks. *Limping! What a cheap trick to get my brother's attention.* Haley glances toward the garage where her brother is washing his car. *Ha! He didn't even notice the neighbor's phony bid for attention.*

A person who is suspicious often thinks things are fishy. She doubts people and questions everything she's told. A suspicious person is skeptical that anything—or anyone—can be trusted. With misgivings about everyone, she puts people's actions and words under a magnifying glass, then often makes false accusations. While it's wise to be careful, don't go overboard and become suspicious of everyone.

Later that day, when Haley tells her mom about the neighbor girl's fake limp, her mom gives her a scolding.

Haley's mom knew something Haley didn't. The neighbor girl had fallen downstairs while holding her baby sister. She'd managed to protect the baby, but she'd badly sprained her own ankle in the process. Haley felt sheepish—and embarrassed at her nasty, suspicious comment. She decided that next time she'd get her facts straight before forming an opinion.

WHAT'S A GIRL TO DO?

Which girls are showing the trait of being suspicious?

- ☐ Mira thanks her friend for the nice birthday gift, but she thinks her friend is giving it to her so she'll write her friend's book report.
- ☐ Cassie hears a boy in her class tell the teacher that he can't find his homework paper and thinks, *What rotten luck.*
- ☐ A boy bumps into Becky pretty hard and says, "Sorry." She replies, "No problem" while thinking, *You did that on purpose!*

CONNECTING TO GOD

Dear Lord, I want to be wise about who to trust—but help me not to be overly suspicious of people. Amen.

more to explore

Their perverted hearts plot evil, and they constantly stir up trouble.

—Proverbs 6:14 (NLT)

I trust in you, LORD; I say, "You are my God." My times
are in your hands.

—Psalm 31:14–15 (TNIV)

You plan to go to a movie with your friend Saturday afternoon, but she cancels to stay home and entertain her
cousin who's coming for the weekend. You go to the movie
alone. Afterward, when exiting the theater, you see your
friend entering by another door with your school friend,
Jeannie. Some out-of-town cousin to entertain! You're hurt
and surprised, but say nothing. Your friend is an honest person, so there must be an explanation. *Lord*, you pray, *please
show me the truth*. When you arrive home, you find a phone
message from your friend. "Hey! My cousin isn't coming
after all. Did you leave already? I'll grab Jeannie and meet
you there." You smile, glad that you trusted your friend.

   A person who is trusting believes what others tell
her. She is unsuspecting, taking what people say "at face
value" instead of thinking they're lying. On the other hand,
a trusting person isn't stupid. She simply gives people the
benefit of the doubt until she has solid evidence that they
can't be trusted. She knows that not everyone in the world
is honest. Jesus understood this about people too. "Jesus

didn't trust them, because he knew human nature. No one needed to tell him what mankind is really like" (John 2:24–25 NLT).

Believers can have a basic trust in others because they have put their real trust in God. They know God will take care of them, regardless of what people may do.

WHAT'S A GIRL TO DO?

Which girls are showing the trait of trusting?

- ☐ Kayla loans her brother money for gas, believing that he'll repay her on Saturday when he gets his paycheck.
- ☐ Rose believes that her friend still likes her, even though she is having a very grouchy day.
- ☐ Libby waits an hour for her ride, figuring her mom is late for a good reason.

CONNECTING TO GOD

Dear Lord, I know I can always trust you to take care of me. Help me to give others the benefit of the doubt. Amen.

more to explore

The Lord is my rock and my fortress and my deliverer; my God, my strength, in whom I will trust.

—Psalm 18:2 (NKJV)

FROM PERFECTIONISM ...

devotion 51

"As for God, his way is perfect; the LORD's word is flawless."

—2 Samuel 22:31 (TNIV)

Jennifer meant well. She worked hard at school, trying to make sure each paper was perfect and each project was flawless. At home, she tried to keep her bedroom spotless, with everything picked up, dusted, and straightened. It was harder at home because she shared a room with her little sister. Jennifer couldn't stand her sister's mess—it kept their room from looking perfect. Once she used a line of masking tape down the middle of the bedroom to divide it in half. It only helped a little because Jennifer could still see her sister's mess. Jennifer couldn't tolerate the disorder. Why couldn't her sister keep their shared space neat? Jennifer tried so hard to avoid mistakes!

Someone who is a perfectionist thinks she must perform without making a single mistake. A perfectionist is concerned about everything being "just so." The perfectionist expects a perfect performance out of herself—and usually everyone else. No person can live up to the perfectionist's standards, including herself. Only God is perfect. Believers *will* one day be perfect—but not till they reach heaven.

108

It's admirable to do a good job, even an excellent job, in all you do. But trying to be perfect—trying to be *God*—sets you up for failure. There's a better way!

WHAT'S A GIRL TO DO?

Which girl is showing the trait of perfectionism?

- ☐ Mira tries on the skirt she made herself in class. When she notices a tiny pucker in the seam, she decides that she'll never wear it.
- ☐ Becky strikes out the first time up to bat, but she spends the remainder of the game cheering on her teammates.
- ☐ Libby tries to control the amount of sugar she eats, but when she gives in and eats one chocolate-chip cookie, she tells herself it is okay to have sugar once in a while.

CONNECTING TO GOD

Dear Lord, help me do my work with excellence but not be so hard on myself or others. Only you are perfect. Amen.

more to explore

You have come to the spirits of the righteous ones in heaven who have now been made perfect.

—Hebrews 12:23 (NLT)

... TO EXCELLENCE

"I have heard of you, that the Spirit of God is in you, and that light and understanding and excellent wisdom are found in you."

—Daniel 5:14 (NKJV)

Some missionaries speak at your church about their work with a community in the Amazon jungle. You're inspired by the Impact they have made while they worked with the people to improve health-care conditions. That alone would have been difficult, but the missionaries set higher, more excellent standards for themselves. They aren't content to stop the spread of disease—they want to raise enough money to build a hospital. They aren't satisfied to teach children how to read—they want to raise enough funds to send several children on to college. They aren't content to do a *good* job. They aim to do an *excellent* job.

A person who works for excellence is someone who tries to do her best. She wants to do quality work, whether at home, at school, or in the community. An exceptional attitude influences how she thinks, speaks, and behaves. She isn't interested in doing barely enough to get by. Instead, she wants to use the gifts God has given her in the best ways possible. However, she stays balanced.

She doesn't go to the other extreme and expect perfection (from herself or others).

We probably can't be excellent in every subject in school, or every sport or activity. Just do things to the best of your ability in those cases. However, excellence should be the standard for every believer when it comes to godly character traits like honesty, patience, and kindness.

WHAT'S A GIRL TO DO?

Which girls are showing the trait of excellence?

- ☐ Kayla rereads the textbook chapter and all her notes before the geography test.
- ☐ Mira takes extra time to frame and mat her photograph for the art fair.
- ☐ Rose studies several books on gardening before digging up her first patch of ground.

CONNECTING TO GOD

Dear Lord, forgive me for the times I've done a sloppy job. Help me to go the extra mile and always do an excellent job. Amen.

more to explore

Daniel distinguished himself ... because an excellent spirit was in him; and the king gave thought to setting him over the whole realm.
—Daniel 6:3 (NKJV)

FROM TALKATIVE . . .

When words are many, sin is not absent, but he who holds his tongue is wise.

—Proverbs 10:19

Alissa met a new girl at the swimming pool. She soon discovered that the new girl would be attending Alissa's school in the fall. Always a friendly girl, Alissa laid her beach towel beside the new girl's. Chatting away, she told her all about the kids in her class, the various activities available, and who the best teachers were. She told the new girl all about her family and how long she had taken swimming lessons. Strolling home that day, Alissa was thrilled that she'd made a new friend. She was glad she'd asked for the girl's phone number. But every time she called, the new girl was too busy to get together. Alissa finally accepted that the new girl didn't want to be her friend, but she had no idea why.

A talkative person may seem very friendly. However, she sometimes rambles on forever—hogging the conversation— and can be very tiresome. Talkative people rarely learn new things from others because they aren't quiet long enough.

Our mouths often get us into trouble, and a talkative person is especially bothered by that problem. Even when saying nice or helpful things, a girl can still talk too much.

People want "give-and-take" in their conversations. Unless you stop talking from time to time, people will think you're not interested in them. So make a conscious effort to be quiet or ask questions instead—and give the other person a chance to answer!

WHAT'S A GIRL TO DO?

Which girls are showing the trait of being talkative?

- ☐ Kayla asks her friend how she likes a book, then without waiting for an answer, tells her how she liked it.
- ☐ Caroline whispers through the movie previews and throughout the main feature, sharing her impressions of the shows.
- ☐ When Becky visits her great-grandmother in the nursing home, she asks, "Can you tell me some more stories about growing up in Wyoming on the ranch?"

CONNECTING TO GOD

Dear Lord, you are such a great listener. I'm glad I may always come to you. Help me be a good listener and good friend to others. Amen.

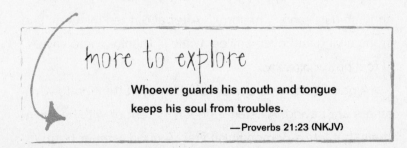

more to explore

Whoever guards his mouth and tongue keeps his soul from troubles.

—Proverbs 21:23 (NKJV)

... TO LISTENER

Everyone should be quick to listen, slow to speak and slow to become angry.

—James 1:19 (TNIV)

You go to the restroom, and on the way back to class, you hear a sniffing sound. Is someone crying? You peek around the corner to the hallway leading to the gym. It's a girl from your homeroom. You don't really know her, but there's obviously something wrong. "Um, can I help?" you ask quietly. Startled to see you, she blushes and stares at the floor. You try again. "You want me to call someone?" She shakes her head. About the time you're ready to give up and leave, words start pouring out. She says her older sister is missing and has probably run away. The girl is terrified that her sister's on drugs and lying dead somewhere. You pray for wisdom about what to say. Your own brother got into trouble a few years ago. Mostly you just say "I know" and "uh-huh" and "I'm sorry." After about ten minutes, she stops crying and even smiles a little. "Thanks," she says. "I feel better already."

A good listener is someone who pays attention to what others are saying. A listener doesn't interrupt with her own ideas, but lets a person finish first. A good listener both hears and understands what others say. A believer especially needs to listen to God and absorb what he says to us in his letter, the Bible.

It's good to share with others when we know things that might be helpful to them. However, sometimes the most helpful thing you can do is to simply care enough to listen. Be quick to listen *first*.

WHAT'S A GIRL TO DO?

Which girl is showing the trait of being a good listener?

- ☐ Cassie never complains about her three-year-old brother's endless bug and snake stories.
- ☐ Lydia asks her dad for directions to the store three times but fails to pay attention to his response.
- ☐ Becky didn't hear the assignment because she was talking to her friend about their after-school plans.

CONNECTING TO GOD

Dear Lord, I want to be a good friend to others. Help me to show that I care by being a good listener. Amen.

more to explore

I will listen to what God the LORD says; he promises peace to his people, his faithful servants.

—Psalm 85:8 (TNIV)

FROM VENGEFUL...

devotion 55

> "Do not seek revenge or bear a grudge against anyone among your people, but love your neighbor as yourself."
>
> —Leviticus 19:18 (TNIV)

Victoria intensely disliked her stepmom. She was so different from Victoria's own mother, who was quiet and never questioned Victoria. Her stepmom, on the other hand, bugged her about everything. One day, while Victoria was at school, her stepmom read her diary and discovered she'd gone to see a movie that she'd been forbidden to see. Victoria's stepmom told her dad, who grounded her for a week. Every day after school Victoria fumed in her bedroom. She plotted ways to pay her stepmom back and still hide it from her dad. She'd find a way to turn the tables and make her stepmom look bad.

A person who is vengeful is unforgiving and spiteful. She wants to settle some score, punishing whoever has hurt her or made her angry. Being *vengeful* means "to seek revenge, to pay someone back for a real or imagined offense."

Whether Victoria was justified or not in being angry with her stepmom, seeking revenge only makes a bad situation worse. The Lord gives us very specific instructions for when we are angry about something done to us. We are to love the other person—not seek revenge. Use kindness as you confront a person who has hurt you or made you angry. Then leave the situation in God's hands.

WHAT'S A GIRL TO DO?

Which girls are showing the trait of being vengeful?

- ☐ Rose finds that her sister has borrowed a book without permission and asks her sister not to do that again.
- ☐ Kayla is irritated because she has to cook supper for the family. To let her family know it wasn't easy for her, she lets the casserole cook too long and burns the meal.
- ☐ Mr. Tinholt tells Becky to be quiet in math class, so she snubs the math teacher the next day when he says hello to her in the hallway.

CONNECTING TO GOD

Dear Lord, it's so tempting to pay people back when they hurt us or make us mad. Help me to love others instead. Amen.

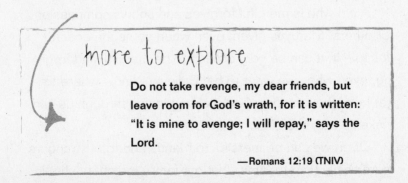

more to explore

Do not take revenge, my dear friends, but leave room for God's wrath, for it is written: "It is mine to avenge; I will repay," says the Lord.

—Romans 12:19 (TNIV)

... TO MERCIFUL

devotion 56

"Be merciful, just as your Father is merciful."
—Luke 6:36 (TNIV)

On Saturday afternoon, you're working on a project for
literature class that is due on Monday. Your little brother
keeps stopping in your room to ask if you'll play with him
even though you have asked him to leave you alone for
a while. Suddenly, you hear your brother yelling outside.
Irritated, you drag yourself to the window overlooking the
backyard and snap, "What's wrong now?" He turns toward
the window, and you see rivulets of tears streaking his
dirty face. "My baseball mitt is gone!" he wails. You sigh,
remembering what it was like to be six years old. "I'll be
out as soon as I put some shoes on," you call. Smiling, you
add, "We'll find it together. I'll play catch with you for a half
hour, and then I need to get my project done."

A girl who is merciful forgives and shows compassion
for others. Mercy is given, even when someone doesn't
deserve it. It can be very difficult to be merciful and forgiving, even when we want to be. Believers know where to
get help, though. Only God working in and through us can
make us truly merciful.

Often we can be merciful to friends and total strangers
more easily than to family. Yet our family members should

118

mean more to us than any other people in the world. This week, practice showing mercy to those you live with. It will cost you some effort to be merciful—in words or in deeds—and give sympathy and comfort to someone. But it will be worth it!

WHAT'S A GIRL TO DO?

Which girl is showing the trait of being merciful?

- ☐ When a girl in play rehearsal messes up her lines—again—Becky wants to roll her eyes along with the other kids. Instead, she smiles encouragingly to the embarrassed girl.
- ☐ Rose notices that her sister used her paints and didn't wash the brushes again. She stomps to her room and tells her sister to never touch her paints again.
- ☐ Cassie sees her father mowing the lawn on a blistering hot day and thinks he's probably very thirsty.

CONNECTING TO GOD

Dear Lord, thank you for all the mercy you've shown me. Help me to care about others more—and show it. Amen.

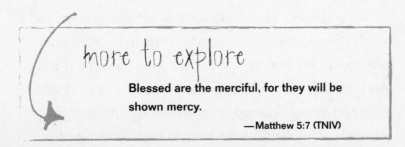

more to explore

Blessed are the merciful, for they will be shown mercy.

—Matthew 5:7 (TNIV)

FROM OUTSPOKEN ...

Those who guard their lips preserve their lives, but those who speak rashly will come to ruin.
—Proverbs 13:3 (TNIV)

Rebecca knew she had good taste in clothes—people said so all the time and even tried to copy her style. So when she went shopping with her friend, she gave her fashion opinions freely. Her friend chose two dresses, some tops, and a pair of jeans to try on. Rebecca marched back to the fitting room with her. When her friend said she didn't need any help, Rebecca brushed her off. "How else will you know if you should buy this stuff?" she asked. During the next half hour, Rebecca passed judgment on the dresses (too frilly), the tops (blah color), and the jeans (okay). Rebecca prided herself on being outspoken, but if you asked her friends, they found her frankness hard to take sometimes.

An outspoken girl is very vocal about her opinions and beliefs. She's straightforward and tends to be blunt when making a point. She may pride herself on speaking plainly and truthfully, but her unrestrained speech is often hurtful.

Being straightforward is a good thing, but taken to extremes, an outspoken girl may do a lot of damage to others. Rebecca needs to learn to speak the truth, but in a loving and kind (instead of pushy) manner.

WHAT'S A GIRL TO DO?

Which girl is showing the trait of being outspoken?

- ☐ While Mira is writing an article about the school dance, she is tempted to say how bad the band was, but she concentrates on how good the food was instead.
- ☐ Though Libby thinks her dad's new tie he received for Father's Day is pretty ugly, she smiles and says nothing.
- ☐ When Kayla sees that her friend is having carrot cake at her birthday party, she starts talking about how much she hates carrot cake because she threw up after eating it once.

CONNECTING TO GOD

Dear Lord, thank you for being kind to me. Help me to watch my tongue and think before I speak—before I hurt someone with my words. Amen.

more to explore

Speaking the truth in love, we will in all things grow up into him who is the head, that is, Christ.

—Ephesians 4:15 (TNIV)

**She opens her mouth with wisdom, and on her tongue
is the law of kindness.**

—Proverbs 31:26 (NKJV)

You're in the audience, waiting for your shy older sister
to play her clarinet solo. When she steps up to the micro-
phone, you hold your breath. Her face is pale, and her
knees shake. She's practiced the solo so much she could
play it in her sleep. Even so, what comes out is painful to
hear. The squeaks make you wince. When she comes in
at the wrong time, it throws her off for several measures.
Your sister's face turns scarlet, and you're embarrassed for
her. The last half of her solo, however, is much better, and
you're relieved. After the concert, you find her in the band
room. She rolls her eyes and asks, "Did you hear all the
squeaks?" You smile and give her a hug. "What I heard,"
you reply, "was a song by my favorite sister." She grins
then and remarks, "I'm your *only* sister. But thanks."

A tactful girl is one who is gracious and well-mannered.
She's sensitive and thoughtful of others' feelings. A person
who's tactful is courteous and discreet. She doesn't blurt
out everything she thinks or knows. She thinks before
she speaks, and if her words might embarrass or hurt

someone, she holds her tongue. Kindness—a fruit of the Spirit—is her guiding principle.

It's important to tell the truth, but you never need to be brutal. We can usually find something truthful to say that is also kind. Being considerate of someone's feelings is usually more important than voicing every opinion we hold. Treat others the way you would like to be treated.

WHAT'S A GIRL TO DO?

Which girls are showing the trait of being tactful?

- ☐ Libby overlooks the burned cookies and compliments her grandma on the great cocoa.
- ☐ When Mira notices that her friend has two big zits on her face, she says nothing.
- ☐ Although Becky thinks her dad's Hawaiian-print shirt is hideous, she tells him that she likes the colors.

CONNECTING TO GOD

Dear Lord, thank you for not pointing out my every mistake. Help me to be just as kind to others. Amen.

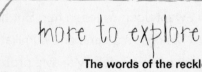

more to explore

The words of the reckless pierce like swords, but the tongue of the wise brings healing.

—Proverbs 12:18 (TNIV)

FROM CALLOUS . . .

A kind man benefits himself, but a cruel man brings trouble on himself.

—Proverbs 11:17

Makayla was very overweight, and every day at school one boy tormented her with cruel comments. Josh's taunts ranged from calling her Rhino and Oinker to Blubber. He pinched the roll of fat around her waist when he walked by her locker. At lunch, he made snorting pig noises as he passed where she ate. Susan, who had the locker next to Makayla's, could see how Josh treated Makayla, but she did nothing. She thought, *What do you expect when you look like an elephant?*

A person who is callous is unfeeling, having no pity for others in distress. Callous people can be hard-hearted and indifferent to others' pain.

Susan may have hardened her heart to Makayla's suffering because she didn't want Josh to tease her. But her callous reaction added to Makayla's shame and humiliation even though she didn't tease her herself. Makayla probably felt she deserved the teasing since everyone seemed to agree with it. When you see someone being bullied, stop it immediately by standing up for that person. No one deserves cruel words.

WHAT'S A GIRL TO DO?

Which girl is showing the trait of callousness?

- ☐ Rose sees a homeless woman begging for food and offers her an apple from her backpack.
- ☐ Becky tells her teacher that she saw two girls pick on a girl in the hall because her clothes were not cool.
- ☐ Grace tells her crying preschool sister to stop acting like a baby.

CONNECTING TO GOD

Dear Lord, thank you for your great care for me. Help me to be more like Jesus and to respond to the needs of others. Amen.

more to explore

Jesus said: "A man was going down from Jerusalem to Jericho, when he fell into the hands of robbers. They ... beat him ... leaving him half dead. A priest ... passed by on the other side. So too, a Levite ... saw him [and] passed by on the other side."

—Luke 10:30–32 (TNIV)

"A new command I give you: Love one another. As I have loved you, so you must love one another. By this everyone will know that you are my disciples, if you love one another."

—John 13:34–35 (TNIV)

It's been a month since your grandmother died. Although others in your family seem back to normal, you notice your mom is still having a rough time. In unguarded moments, you catch her despairing looks as she stares out the window. One evening, only you and your mom are at home. "How are you feeling?" you ask while you do dishes together. She says, "Fine," but it doesn't ring true. "I miss Nana," you finally say. "I miss how she used to read to me and tell me stories about her childhood." You pause, then ask, "What do you miss the most?" Your mom sighs, speaks slowly at first, then the memories come rushing out. Through laughter and tears, for the next hour, she shares special memories of her mother. At the end of the evening, your mom seems more at peace.

A sensitive person is sympathetic to others' feelings and problems. Kind and considerate, she is keenly aware of how others feel, and she responds accordingly. Her heart is easily touched, and she tries to think of ways to help people through tough times. When others are in pain, the sensitive girl hurts with them.

It can be awkward when someone you care about is hurting. Sometimes there's not much you can do except give a hug or a kind word—or just listen. And yet, that often means a great deal—and is very much appreciated.

WHAT'S A GIRL TO DO?

Which girls are showing the trait of sensitivity?

- ☐ At the library, a little boy looks up from his book with a panicked look. He can't see his mom or dad. Libby watches him to make sure he finds them before she goes back to her own reading.
- ☐ A new girl is sitting alone at recess again. Cassie wonders why she doesn't make more of an effort to make friends.
- ☐ In ballet class, when another dancer keeps bumping into Kayla, Kayla asks her kindly if she is feeling okay.

CONNECTING TO GOD

Dear Lord, thank you for the people in my life who are kind to me. Help me be sensitive to their needs as well. Amen.

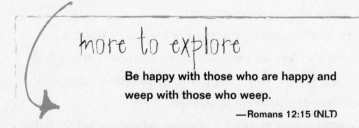

more to explore

Be happy with those who are happy and weep with those who weep.

—Romans 12:15 (NLT)

Lazy people irritate their employers like vinegar to the teeth or smoke in the eyes.

—Proverbs 10:26 (NLT)

Courtney babysat for two children after school: a first grader and a third grader. She was supposed to feed them a healthy snack of fruit and cheese and then help them with homework, using their math flash cards and listening to them read. After they finished that, they could go outside and play games or go to the park. No TV or junk food was allowed after school. At first Courtney stuck to the rules, but she tired of them quickly. She preferred talking on the phone to her friends, so she parked the kids in front of cartoons with some cookies, reminding them that it was "their secret." Courtney was always busy helping with homework when their mother arrived home, though. She thought the mother's expectations were too high, and Courtney didn't see the point of working so hard.

A person whose standards are mediocre does a job that is barely okay, or passable. It's ordinary, nothing special, or just so-so. The most common reason a person does a mediocre, careless job is laziness.

Courtney was surprised one day when the kids' mother came home early from work with a bad headache.

She found them eating ice cream in front of the TV while watching cartoons. That was Courtney's last day on the job.

WHAT'S A GIRL TO DO?

Which girls are making a mediocre effort?

- ☐ Cassie has to write a report on a local museum. She does all her research on the Internet because visiting the site or interviewing someone is too much work.
- ☐ After school, Libby is supposed to grate cheese and cut up veggies for homemade pizza. Her dad made the crust ahead of time. Instead, Libby gets out a frozen pizza and adds olives.
- ☐ Mira wants to qualify for the cross-country track team in the fall and practices all summer to get into good shape.

CONNECTING TO GOD

Dear Lord, it's so tempting to do just enough to get by. I know you didn't create me to be mediocre. Please help me to become an excellent young woman. Amen.

more to explore

Never be lazy, but work hard and serve the Lord enthusiastically.
—Romans 12:11 (NLT)

... TO OUTSTANDING

"Many daughters have done well, but you excel them all."

—Proverbs 31:29 (NKJV)

Your youth group's car wash to raise money for the home-less shelter has cars waiting in a long line. "Hurry along!" the youth pastor calls. You glance sideways at your friends working on a minivan and see them speed up. When the minivan pulls away ten minutes later, its hubcaps are still muddy, and soap streaks show down the back glass. You wonder how happy the owner will be when he arrives home. You speed up too, but you decide to do the same quality of job. You continue scrubbing the cars clean, dig-ging bugs out of grilles, and thoroughly rinsing off the soap. You don't finish as many cars as your friends, but you're proud of your work.

A girl who does outstanding work has high standards. She doesn't settle for less than her best. She has excellent moral values, and she uses her God-given gifts and talents to the best of her ability. Everything she does is first-rate, done with quality in mind.

Doing an exceptional job in everything can be hard unless you learn to do everything with Jesus as your "audience." Others won't always appreciate when you take your time and do a thorough, quality job. Your boss might only want the job done fast. Try, in everything you do, to give high quality anyway. The Lord will notice.

WHAT'S A GIRL TO DO?

Which girl is showing the trait of making an outstanding effort?

- ☐ After Rose bakes cookies, she washes the baking dishes and cleans up the kitchen.
- ☐ When Mira helps the librarian after school, she reshelves books in the right section wherever she can find an empty spot on the shelf.
- ☐ Becky mows the front lawn very well, but skips the grass behind the garage where no one can see it.

CONNECTING TO GOD

Dear Lord, give me a desire to produce high-quality work, even if no one except you is looking. Thank you for giving me the strength to go the extra mile. Amen.

more to explore

"Now, my daughter, do not fear. I will do for you whatever you ask, for all my people in the city know that you are a woman of excellence."

—Ruth 3:11 (NASB)

FROM MISLEADING ...

You love evil rather than good, falsehood rather than speaking the truth. You love every harmful word, you deceitful tongue!

—Psalm 52:3–4 (TNIV)

Sierra's teacher complimented her on her report for careers class. "You must be proud of your dad's work at the hospital," she said.

Sierra nodded and replied, "I just wish he didn't have to work such long hours. But emergencies happen."

"How true!" said her teacher. "Last week my daughter fell off her bike and broke her collarbone. I'm sure we made our doctor late for his supper."

Sierra shrugged and said, "It's all in a day's work." She headed home, feeling slightly guilty that her teacher assumed her dad was a doctor. He wasn't, and her careers report hadn't said so. She'd only written about the operating room and all the instruments needed for surgeries. She knew about it from her dad, who sterilized instruments. If the teacher mistakenly thought he was a doctor, Sierra couldn't help it.

A person who misleads someone is being deceptive. She can lead you astray with sly cunning or by leaving out important information. A person who is misleading often tries to trick you into doing or thinking something. However "nicely" it's done, being misleading is still dishonest.

Don't give a misleading impression on purpose. It's called lying. If you mislead someone accidentally, correct it when you discover it. The truth has a way of coming out, and when your deception is discovered, people will find it very hard to trust you again.

WHAT'S A GIRL TO DO?

Which girls are showing the trait of being misleading?

- ☐ Kayla tells her dad she is going to the library, which she is, but she doesn't mention that her stop is on the way to the mall.
- ☐ Libby contributes a plate of cookies to a bake sale, but she admits buying them at a bakery.
- ☐ Cassie borrows her sister's jacket, and when she's complimented on her new coat, she smiles and says thanks.

CONNECTING TO GOD

Dear Lord, forgive me for the times I've told only part of the truth. Help me not give in to the temptation to look better than I am. Amen.

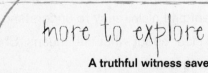

more to explore

A truthful witness saves lives, but a false witness is deceitful.

—Proverbs 14:25 (TNIV)

... TO STRAIGHTFORWARD

"All you need to say is simply 'Yes,' or 'No.'"
—Matthew 5:37 (TNIV)

You're home alone when the doorbell rings. You answer
the door to find a young girl selling boxes of Girl Scout
cookies. You're the only person you know who doesn't
like Girl Scout cookies, but you hate to turn her down.
You're tempted to say you already bought several boxes
from someone else. Or that you're diabetic and can't eat
sugar. Or that you'd buy some if you hadn't already spent
your allowance. But you have a bad habit of lying to keep
people from getting upset with you. Lately you've been
trying to break that habit. So when the little girl asks you
to buy some cookies, you take a deep breath and say, "I'm
sorry, but I need to say no today." The little girl looks disappointed for a moment, then says, "Okay. Bye."

To be a straightforward girl means to be honest and
frank, speaking in an upfront manner and not hiding things.
This girl's speech is direct and plain, easy to understand.
A straightforward girl is clear about what she means. She
isn't blunt or hurtful—just honest.

Sometimes it's hard to be direct with people, especially
if we're afraid they won't like what we have to say.

Someone might become angry at our comment or be hurt by it. Take the risk and be honest anyway. Lying is still lying. Instead of lying, look for ways to be truthful, yet kind.

WHAT'S A GIRL TO DO?

Which girls are showing the trait of being straightforward?

- ☐ Cassie says to her teacher, "I'd rather study Edison than Betsy Ross for my report—is that okay?"
- ☐ Becky really wants a gift certificate from a CD store for her birthday. When someone asks what she wants, she says, "Oh, nothing."
- ☐ Libby looks at everything on the menu and says, "I'd like the shrimp if it isn't too expensive."

CONNECTING TO GOD

Dear Lord, you know how hard it is for me to say exactly what I mean sometimes. Give me courage to speak up, yet be truthful and kind at the same time. Amen.

more to explore

Honesty guides good people; dishonesty destroys treacherous people.

—Proverbs 11:3 (NLT)

Everything is wearisome beyond description. No matter how much we see, we are never satisfied.

—Ecclesiastes 1:8 (NLT)

Jordan yawned through her entire American history class. She wasn't tired—she'd had nine hours of sleep the night before. She was just plain bored. What difference did it make what a bunch of guys did two hundred years ago? It had nothing to do with her today. Jordan couldn't see the point of studying history—or anything else lately, for that matter. She was weary of school and tests and book reports. Her teachers were dull. The subjects were even duller. Jordan just didn't care about school anymore.

Someone who is bored is feeling weary and dull. There is a humdrum flatness to life, and the bored person finds life tedious and tiresome. Nothing seems very interesting. Everything feels stale. A bored person feels halfhearted and indifferent to life.

Our daily lives are full of things that seem boring, yet need to be done. We get weary of many things: doing chores at home, studying school assignments, working hard at sports practice—even the sameness of attending church. Is being bored something that simply happens to a girl, something beyond her control? Surprisingly, the answer is no. Whether or not we find something boring depends on the attitude we bring to the activity. Don't be passively bored. Instead, take action! What can you do to make each necessary activity more interesting or fun? Could you play loud music while you clean your room? Or do your studying on a blanket under your apple tree? Take steps to breathe more life and interest into your daily routine.

WHAT'S A GIRL TO DO?

Which girls are showing the trait of boredom?

- ☐ Rose pokes through her salad at supper, tuning out her parents' conversation.
- ☐ During the church sermon, Kayla plans her outfits for the week.
- ☐ During free reading time, Becky pulls out a book that she's anxious to read.

CONNECTING TO GOD

Dear Lord, I don't want to be bored with the great life you've given me. Please restore my enthusiasm for (fill in your own activity). Amen.

more to explore

Our great desire is that you will ... not become spiritually dull and indifferent.
—Hebrews 6:11–12 (NLT)

... TO ENTHUSIASTIC

Work with enthusiasm, as though you were working for the Lord rather than for people.

—Ephesians 6:7 (NLT)

You have always loved your family's traditions at Christmas. Since your mom got remarried last summer, you know the traditions will be changing because your stepfather's family has traditions of their own. Your mom seems worried that you will feel bad because things won't be the same. Part of you feels sad and wouldn't mind skipping Christmas altogether. But you really want to help make the new family work. One night your stepdad announces that you're all going to one of those cut-your-own-Christmas-tree farms. It wasn't one of your traditions or theirs—it is something new for everyone. You almost say, "Mom, do I have to go?" But you look at the faces of your stepsister and brother and say cheerfully, "We've never done that before. Sounds like fun." Your biggest surprise comes two hours later after cutting the white pine while sipping hot chocolate and laughing in the tree shed: You all had a great time—and you hope it becomes part of your new Christmas traditions.

An enthusiastic person is eager and interested in life. There is a wholehearted, spirited involvement with others. Passionate feelings stir the enthusiastic person.

Enthusiasm is catching, so it's wonderful to have an enthusiastic friend or family member.

Certain activities we enjoy fill us with enthusiasm. Other times—out of love for others—we may need to *choose* to be enthusiastic until our feelings catch up.

WHAT'S A GIRL TO DO?

Which girls are showing the trait of enthusiasm?

- ☐ Becky prefers to play softball, but even while "warming the bench," she yells and cheers for her teammates.
- ☐ Cassie sighs throughout the church service, gazes around the sanctuary, and refuses to sing the songs.
- ☐ Mira looks at the new curtains her mom made for the living room and says, "Cool colors, Mom! They really brighten up the room."

CONNECTING TO GOD

Dear Lord, forgive me for sometimes being such a downer to others. Help my enthusiasm lift people up wherever I go. Amen.

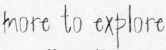

more to explore

**You excel in so many ways—in your faith,...
your enthusiasm, and your love for us.**
—2 Corinthians 8:7 (NLT)

FROM DOUBLE-MINDED ...

> The one who doubts is like a wave of the sea, blown
> and tossed by the wind ... They are double-minded
> and unstable in all they do.
>
> —James 1:6, 8 (TNIV)

Maria couldn't decide what to do about her friend, Jenna.
They were both twelve, but Jenna had a boyfriend in *high
school*. Maria couldn't believe it. She and Jenna were in
the same youth group, and Maria knew Jenna's parents
from church. They'd be sick with worry if they knew Jenna
was dating anyone, let alone a boy so much older. Although
she'd been sworn to secrecy, Maria was having second
thoughts. For one thing, Jenna had let it slip that she'd
been drinking a little and smoking too. Maria went back
and forth, trying to make the right decision. One day she
thought it was her duty as Jenna's friend to tell someone
about Jenna's secret life. The next day Maria decided that
Jenna was responsible for her own actions. Making up her
mind what to do—if anything—was driving Maria crazy.

A double-minded person has two ways of thinking. She
goes back and forth, believing one thing, then another. A
double-minded girl gets confused when trying to make a
decision and stick to it. Her mind feels muddled and dis-
ordered instead of clear, as she wavers and waffles with
indecision. How frustrating!

There's really only one answer to being double-minded. Discover, through prayer and reading God's Word and waiting for guidance, what God has to say about your situation. Then, follow God's instructions and leave the consequences to him.

WHAT'S A GIRL TO DO?

Which girls are showing the trait of being double-minded?

- ◯ Mira cannot decide which sports team to join; she waits till the last minute, finally flipping a coin to decide.
- ◯ Cassie takes two hours in the mall shopping for her friend's birthday present. She goes round and round between a shirt, a CD, and a book.
- ◯ Rose reads through the menu, thinks a moment, and then orders her sandwich.

CONNECTING TO GOD

Dear Lord, I'm tired of wavering back and forth when making decisions. Help me to think clearly, and show me your will. Amen.

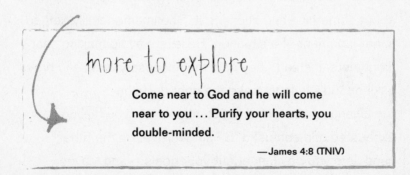

more to explore

Come near to God and he will come near to you ... Purify your hearts, you double-minded.

—James 4:8 (TNIV)

... TO DECISIVE

"How long will you waver between two opinions?"
—1 Kings 18:21 (TNIV)

Like your friends, you want to go out for band. Most of them chose the flute because the tiny case is easy to carry around. You want to sit with them in band, but after trying several instruments, you really love the trombone. Making those deep sliding notes is fun! Unfortunately, the whole trombone section is filled with boys. *Ugh!* And yet ... the idea of playing the trombone just thrills you, no matter how odd your friends think it is. After praying about it, you follow your heart and rent a trombone. Although the first weeks of practice are hard, you don't regret the decision.

Someone who is decisive is certain and firm. After taking time to consider her choices, she makes up her mind about something and sticks to it. She is emotionally settled in her judgment of a situation. Believers avoid making snap judgments. Instead, they gain the necessary facts and pray, asking God's help to make the right decision.

Changing your mind constantly leaves you feeling exhausted and confused. Being decisive, on the other hand, lets you be clear about your goals—and leaves you with energy to pursue them. In order to make good

decisions—to make the *right* choices—you must allow
God to guide you, through prayer and reading the Bible. It
is no good to be decisive unless you make good decisions!

WHAT'S A GIRL TO DO?

Which girls are showing the trait of decisiveness?

☐ Rose goes to the store and chooses a yellow paint
to match a fabric sample, returns home, and paints
her bedroom.

☐ After Libby researches running shoes online to
find the best kind for her wide feet, she hunts for a
shoe store carrying that brand.

☐ Cassie wants to plant flowers outside her window.
She wanders through acres of plants at the garden
shop but returns home without buying anything.

CONNECTING TO GOD

Dear Lord, being unable to make decisions wastes a lot of
my time. Help me to rely on you in all my decision making.
Amen.

more to explore

**"No one can serve two masters. Either you
will hate the one and love the other, or you
will be devoted to the one and despise the
other."**

—Matthew 6:24 (TNIV)

FROM QUITTER ...

devotion 64

> Let us not become weary in doing good, for at
> the proper time we will reap a harvest if we do
> not give up.
>
> —Galatians 6:9 (TNIV)

Savannah's family was moving across the country from
Tennessee to California. It was Savannah's responsibility
to pack everything in her bedroom, and she started plenty
of times. One day she packed two small boxes—before
she found her old diary and sat down and read it for hours.
Another time she cleaned under her bed—until she found
her old ballet shoes and gave up packing to practice her
dance steps. One day she tried on all her shorts and swim-
wear, but forgot to pack anything. Savannah's mom grew
irritated when Savannah wouldn't stick to the job and left
so much packing unfinished.

Quitters are people who give up easily. They withdraw
from difficult people, boring jobs, and hard times. Rather
than hang on, they relinquish their hold and abandon those
who count on them. Quitters stick around when it's easy,
but they make poor friends because you can't count on
them during difficult times.

A girl who can't seem to finish what she starts needs to
pray for help in developing endurance. Without that quality,

important things don't get finished. You can't be successful at school or with important relationships unless you're able to endure hard things and finish what you start.

WHAT'S A GIRL TO DO?

Which girls are showing the trait of being a quitter?

☐ Rose completes half of her math homework before bedtime. She intends to finish the other half in the morning but doesn't make time.

☐ Kayla decides to ride her bike across town to her friend's house, and because it's so windy, it takes fifteen minutes longer than she expected.

☐ Mira is tired of reading the book she chose for her book report, so she reads the first two chapters and skips to the last page to see how it ends.

CONNECTING TO GOD

Dear Lord, I get mad at myself when I give up and quit. Help me to forgive myself but also to stick to things until I'm finished. Amen.

more to explore

Jesus told his disciples a parable to show them that they should always pray and not give up.

—Luke 18:1 (TNIV)

... TO ENDURING

We are pressed on every side by troubles, but we are not crushed. We are perplexed, but not driven to despare.

—2 Corinthians 4:8 (NLT)

You're thrilled when your neighbor gives you a weekend job washing windows at his car dealership. The entire front and both sides of the showroom are glass, and he promises to pay you ten dollars per hour. The first day is tiring, but not bad. It's a bright, sunny day. For three hours you climb up and down a stepladder, polishing the showroom windows till they gleam. The next weekend, though, is miserable. The temperature is in the forties; the wind whips your hair in your eyes, and your red, chapped hands ache. You're determined to finish, though. By the time you head home with forty dollars in your pocket, you're frozen through, but proud of finishing a tough job.

A person who is enduring has "grit" or guts to stick things out to the end. An enduring person is hardy and can withstand pressure without giving up. A girl with an enduring nature survives and rises above situations that others find too hard. The ability for a believer to endure things— *and with a good attitude*—comes from the Lord. He's our strength when we're weak.

Many people try to endure by relying on their own abilities. By ourselves, our willpower and determination won't get us very far. Asking for God's help to endure will keep us standing firm to the end.

WHAT'S A GIRL TO DO?

Which girls are showing the trait of endurance?

- ☐ Libby signs up for a summer computer class, but she drops out after two weeks because it isn't much fun.
- ☐ Becky sets a new year's resolution to eat healthier. She writes down everything she eats and sticks to the USDA pyramid guidelines for sixteen weeks in order to make it a habit
- ☐ Kayla joins the track team and stays with it the whole season, despite spraining her ankle twice.

CONNECTING TO GOD

Dear Lord, I know that your love endures forever. Help me develop endurance in many areas of my life. Please give me your strength. Amen.

more to explore

Those who hope in the LORD will renew their strength. They will soar on wings like eagles; they will run and not grow weary, they will walk and not be faint.

—Isaiah 40:31 (TNIV)

FROM COMPLAINING ...

Do everything without complaining and arguing.
—Philippians 2:14 (NLT)

Chelsea's older sister could finally drive, and one of her
chores was grocery shopping for the family. On Saturday,
Chelsea went with her sister to buy the weekly groceries.
Her sister griped all the way to the store about the inter-
ruption to her afternoon nap, the stupid drivers who cut her
off, the car heater not working right, the crowded parking
lot, the crooked grocery cart wheels, and a dozen other
inconveniences she was experiencing. By the time they
checked out and headed home, Chelsea couldn't wait to
get away from her sister. She longed for peace and quiet.
Chelsea's life wasn't perfect either, but she'd already
learned that complaining about it only made her feel worse.

People with the habit of complaining like to gripe
and grumble. They can raise a fuss and bellyache about
anything. They find fault with people, places, and circumstances. Being around complaining people for very long is
exhausting. They aren't satisfied with anything and put a
damper on other people's enjoyment.

Complaining can become a bad habit. Finding fault with
everything is very draining on both the person doing the

complaining and those forced to listen to it. Pray for God's help to break this habit. Make a decision today that you'll stop complaining—and look for something positive to say instead.

WHAT'S A GIRL TO DO?

Which girl is showing the trait of being a complainer?

☐ Libby drops many hints that she wants a scooter for Christmas. When she doesn't receive one, she keeps her disappointment to herself.

☐ Becky walks into the house after softball practice, sniffs the air, makes a face, and says, "We're not having spaghetti *again*, are we?"

☐ Rose notices her little brother left fingerprints on the computer screen again while playing his video game and wipes them off without a word.

CONNECTING TO GOD

Dear Lord, it's so easy to be self-centered and complain when things don't go my way. Help me to focus on you and keep quiet instead. Amen.

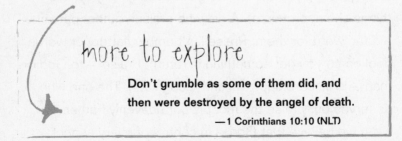

more to explore

**Don't grumble as some of them did, and
then were destroyed by the angel of death.**

—1 Corinthians 10:10 (NLT)

From birth I have relied on you; you brought me forth from my mother's womb. I will ever praise you.

—Psalm 71:6 (TNIV)

Your mom received a promotion at work, but it means you'll be moving to another state. It feels like the end of the world. You've attended only one school in your life, and you've had the same best friend since kindergarten. Lately in Sunday school, however, you've been learning about praising God no matter what your circumstances. You realize that God is in control—and that he has a good plan for your life. Taking a deep breath, you pray, *Lord, I don't understand why this is happening. I know you love me, and that I can trust you. I choose to praise you for this move. Amen.* A deep peace you didn't expect settles over you.

A praising girl is one who gives credit freely for the things she approves of. A girl who praises others puts in a good word for them. Praise isn't empty flattery or words spoken so you get something in return. Praise—to God or man—is sincere approval and recognition. The one who deserves our praise the most is our heavenly Father.

If we believe that God is in control of every aspect of our lives—and that God is love—we can praise him no matter what happens. He allows things for only good purposes (Romans 8:28). Learn to praise God for everything—and everyone—he has allowed or placed in your life. You will then find it easier to praise people as well.

WHAT'S A GIRL TO DO?

Which girls are demonstrating praise?

☐ Libby tells her friend what a beautiful job she's done on her art project.

☐ When Kayla finds out that she's dropped from the softball team, she thanks God anyway for the chance to try out.

☐ Cassie looks at the gorgeous sunset and thanks God for the beauty.

CONNECTING TO GOD

Dear Lord, there are so many things to praise you for every day. Forgive me when I forget! Amen.

more to explore

They sang responsively, praising and giving thanks to the LORD: "For He is good, for His mercy endures forever."

—Ezra 3:11 (NKJV)

From HARSHNESS ...

**A gentle answer turns away wrath, but a harsh word
stirs up anger.**

—Proverbs 15:1 (TNIV)

On Saturday Shelby and her little sister were assigned
to weed the flower gardens in the front yard. Shelby had
shown her sister four times already what plants were weeds
and which ones were baby marigolds and petunias. When
Shelby went inside for a drink of water, she also glanced
through a magazine before heading back outside. Out front,
she was horrified to see the patch by the sidewalk her
sister had weeded alone. Clusters of weeds stood tall and
healthy, while a little pile of wilting marigold plants lay in a
heap on the grass. "I don't believe it!" Shelby yelled. "How
many times do I have to show you which ones are weeds?"
She held up the limp marigold plants. "You just pulled up
Mom's flowers, you idiot. Are you blind? You're gonna be in
so much trouble. What's the matter with you?"

Harshness means that a person is "cruel in her words
and actions." A harsh person is rough and sharp, spewing
unpleasant and unfeeling words at people. Her speech has
no mercy; it could even be called brutal. Harshness can do
long-term damage to others.

As believers, we must stop ourselves from blurting out the harsh or cruel things we sometimes think. It takes self-discipline to guard our words. Self-discipline (or self-control) is a fruit of the Holy Spirit. Make a decision today to treat others in a kind manner—the same way you'd like to be treated.

WHAT'S A GIRL TO DO?

Which girls are showing the trait of harshness?

☐ Kayla enters the living room where her brother is sitting on the couch. She deliberately stomps on her brother's foot and says, "Move, turkey."

☐ Cassie glances at the cookies her sister made— and burned—and says, "You've been busy this afternoon."

☐ Evie shakes her head when she sees her big brother's haircut and exclaims, "Loser."

CONNECTING TO GOD

Dear Lord, help me forgive those who have been harsh with me. Help me to never be cruel or harsh with others. Amen.

more to explore

Get rid of all bitterness, rage, anger, harsh words, and slander, as well as all types of evil behavior.

—Ephesians 4:31 (NLT)

... TO GENTLENESS

The fruit of the Spirit is ... gentleness.
—Galatians 5:22–23 (TNIV)

You're laughing with your friends from Sunday school class while you all head to the restroom before church. As you reach for the door handle, it opens abruptly and hits you in the arm. Hard. An older girl blinks in surprise, but she doesn't apologize. "Excuse me," you say, even though you honestly think it's the other girl's fault for not being careful. She raises one eyebrow, looks down at you, and says, "You should watch where you're going." A cutting remark comes quickly to your tongue, but you bite it back, fighting the irritation that rises in you. You force yourself to smile instead. "Yes, you're right," you say. Later, sitting in church, you're glad your temper didn't explode, as it's done in the past. Instead, your gentle answer helped avoid a nasty scene.

Gentleness is the trait of being kind and soft toward others. A gentle person is tender and agreeable, ready to make peace. A believer is expected to be gentle, as Jesus was, but we can't do it—at least not for long—by ourselves. We need the power of the Holy Spirit working in us daily. He will smooth off our rough edges and change our natural harshness into gentleness.

It's easy to be gentle, peaceable, and kind when life is running smoothly and no one is bugging us. The real test of our gentleness is when we're being treated harshly. Can you respond to unfair treatment or irritating circumstances with gentleness? You can—if you ask the Holy Spirit to help.

WHAT'S A GIRL TO DO?

Which girls are showing the trait of gentleness?

- ☐ Mira works in the nursery, rocking and singing to babies during the church service.
- ☐ Cassie visits her grandmother in the hospital and sits by the bed, holding her grandma's hand while she sleeps.
- ☐ Becky hears her sister crying in her room and thinks, *I wonder what the big baby is bawling about now.*

CONNECTING TO GOD

Dear Lord, thank you for always being gentle with me. Help me treat others with the same kind of gentle kindness. Amen.

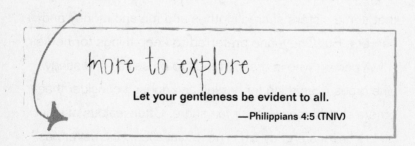

more to explore

Let your gentleness be evident to all.

—Philippians 4:5 (TNIV)

The greedy stir up dissension, but those who trust in the LORD will prosper.

—Proverbs 28:25 (TNIV)

Cheyenne was the oldest child in the family, and she felt that gave her certain rights. She expected first choice on most things, and usually she took whatever she wanted. After school, she ate all ten cookies left in the cookie jar. She didn't share the family computer even when her sister needed to use it for a school project. When Christmas money arrived from Grandma—money to be shared by both girls—Cheyenne bought a new video phone. Technically it was for both girls, but Cheyenne took the phone to school and her sister never got to use it. Cheyenne knew her sister wished things were different. She knew that some sisters shared clothes and fun and money and secrets. But Cheyenne preferred to keep things for herself.

A person who is greedy tends to be selfish and stingy. She grabs everything for herself and doesn't consider that others should receive their fair share. Often jealous of what others have, a greedy girl is never satisfied. She never has enough things, enough food, enough money, or enough compliments. Her attitude is one of extreme self-centeredness.

If you're greedy—always wanting more—ask the Lord to help you be content with what you have.

Rather than greedy, followers of Jesus are called to be focused on other people. We are to divide up what we have and be "ready to give, willing to share" (1 Timothy 6:18 NKJV).

WHAT'S A GIRL TO DO?

Which girls are showing the trait of being greedy?

☐ Rose cuts the candy bar into equal parts, then takes one piece for herself.

☐ Libby grabs the remote control for the TV and hangs on to it all evening.

☐ Grace barely eats any supper because she is talking about herself the entire time, keeping everyone at the table focused on her.

CONNECTING TO GOD

Dear Lord, forgive me for thinking of myself first and wanting the biggest share of things. Help me to think of others first. Amen.

more to explore

Greedy people try to get rich quick but don't realize they're headed for poverty.

—Proverbs 28:22 (NLT)

.. TO GENEROUS

Remember this: Whoever sows sparingly will also reap sparingly, and whoever sows generously will also reap generously.

—**2 Corinthians 9:6 (TNIV)**

When your bus pulls into the school parking lot, your little brother grabs your arm. "I forgot my lunch," he wails. Luckily, after checking the school menu that morning, you packed a lunch. It has all your favorite things in it: a big container of green grapes, two chocolate-chip cookies, the last corn chips in the bag, and some cold pizza.

You pat your brother's arm. "Don't worry," you say. "You can have some of mine." To be honest, you wish you could keep your whole lunch. Your brother's eyes light up when you unzip your insulated bag. Wrapping up half of everything, you put it in your brother's backpack. You won't get full at lunch now, but your brother will have something.

A generous person is a giving person. She is unselfish, thinking of others before herself. She is bighearted and openhanded with things she owns. She gives without counting the cost or expecting anything in return. A generous believer feels rich in the blessings she's received from God and wants to be generous with others in return.

Compared to the people in most countries of the world, we Americans are rich. Most of us have a good home, enough food to eat, and plenty of clothes to wear. Many of us eat *too* much and have enough clothes for *half a dozen* people. We need to care about the needs of others—and give from a generous heart.

WHAT'S A GIRL TO DO?

Which girls are showing the trait of generosity?

- ☐ Libby gives away toys and clothes she hasn't used in a year to hurricane victims.
- ☐ Mira counts her dollars and then drops a dime in the Salvation Army bucket at Christmas.
- ☐ Rose gives a dollar at church every week out of her five-dollar allowance.

CONNECTING TO GOD

Dear Lord, thank you for taking such good care of me. Help me to be generous with others. Amen.

more to explore

I am praying that you will put into action the generosity that comes from your faith as you understand and experience all the good things we have in Christ.

—Philemon verse 6 (NLT)

From GROUCHY ...

Don't grumble against one another, brothers and sisters, or you will be judged.

—James 5:9 (TNIV)

Tiffany was nicknamed "Oscar the Grouch" when in kindergarten. Even at age twelve, her dad called her Oscar several times per week. Tiffany scowled so much her forehead was creased already. She complained about the choices of breakfast cereal in the morning. Daily she found fault with the weather. (A rainy day meant she'd have to get wet, but a sunny day meant she would be hot.) Tiffany was often irritated with her friend Beth. Beth either called too often (and bothered Tiffany) or didn't call enough (which meant she didn't care enough about Tiffany). If there wasn't anything to complain about, Tiffany invented something. Her grouchy habit was well practiced.

A person who is grouchy is a complainer and a faultfinder. A grouchy girl grumbles constantly, and nothing suits her crabby disposition. She whines her way through her days. It is difficult to enjoy being around this testy, surly person. She often has trouble keeping friends.

Grouchy people *do* get a lot of attention. Others often try to make them happy or fix whatever the grouch is complaining about. Over time, however, grouches end up alone. For most people, they are too negative to enjoy— and too much work! So don't be a thundercloud. Choose to bring sunshine into the lives of others instead.

WHAT'S A GIRL TO DO?

Which girls are showing the trait of grouchiness?

- ☐ Kayla goes bowling with her family, tries a dozen balls, but says there's something wrong with them all.
- ☐ Lydia holds the new puppy, which won't stop wiggling and licking her arm. This makes her so mad, she drops the dog in the grass.
- ☐ Cascio shares the backseat with her sister on their vacation trip to the Rockies. She gets irritated when her sister looks at her. Several times a day, she snaps, "Stop looking at me!"

CONNECTING TO GOD

Dear Lord, I don't want to be a grouchy girl that people want to avoid. Help me to look at the bright side of life— and share it with others. Amen.

more to explore

If you keep on biting and devouring each other, watch out or you will be destroyed by each other.

—Galatians 5:15 (TNIV)

... TO GOOD-NATURED

A cheerful heart is good medicine, but a crushed spirit dries up the bones.

—Proverbs 17:22 (TNIV)

You and another girl are paired on a team on Environmental Appreciation Day. Your assignment is to clean up the football field where trash and litter have blown in. The November day is windy and damp, overcast and gloomy—not exactly a fun day to be outside. Your teammate is a shy girl; you don't remember her ever talking in class. Working with her might be more of a challenge than the weather. When you're both halfway across the field, it starts to sprinkle. "Lucky for us we have extra garbage bags," you say. She watches in surprise as you turn a bag upside down, tear openings for your head and arms, and then pull it on over your clothes. "Here. I'll make you one too," you say. Then, whistling a tune from your favorite movie, you continue to bag up the litter.

A good-natured person is easygoing and cheerful, pleasant to get along with, kind and agreeable. Goodness is a trait developed in believers by the Holy Spirit.

It's not easy to be even-tempered and good-natured when things don't go the way you planned. But if you're a follower of Jesus and have the Holy Spirit living and working in you, then you can stay agreeable in the most disagreeable circumstances. On our own, we can be pretty grouchy. With the Holy Spirit in control, however, we can be transformed. Ask for the Lord's help.

WHAT'S A GIRL TO DO?

Which girls are showing the trait of being good-natured?

☐ When the teacher passes out the test with a different grade than Kayla expects, she slams the test down on her desk, folds her arms angrily, and scowls for all to see.

☐ When Libby slips on the ice and falls, she scrambles to her feet, grins, and takes a bow.

☐ While babysitting, Cassie sings song after song to a toddler who is afraid of the sound of the wind and rain hitting the house.

CONNECTING TO GOD

Dear Lord, thank you for all the good-natured people in my life. Help me to put forth extra effort and be more positive myself. Amen.

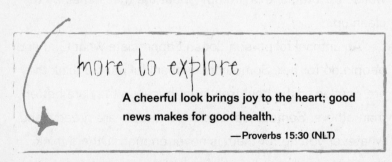

more to explore

A cheerful look brings joy to the heart; good news makes for good health.
—**Proverbs 15:30 (NLT)**

FROM UNTHANKFUL . . .

Although they knew God, they neither glorified him as God nor gave thanks to him.

—Romans 1:21 (TNIV)

For Jade's birthday party, she chooses a combination swimming-and-slumber party for six of her friends. First, Jade's mom and dad barbecue hot dogs and hamburgers for them. Then the girls go swimming before Jade cuts the cake and opens gifts. Jade receives clothes, a couple of DVDs, and a music CD from her parents. She gets similar gifts from her friends. Her mom fixes pizza for the girls at midnight. The next morning, Jade's parents give the overnighters a ride home. Jade, exhausted, crashes on the couch to sleep all day. She does all this without saying "thank you" for the gifts or the work her parents did for the party. When she wakes up later, she is grumpy about the mess she has to clean up.

An unthankful person doesn't appreciate what God and people do for her. Sometimes unthankful people think they are entitled to the best treatment because they are better than others. Sometimes unthankful people are greedy, and whatever you do for them is never enough. Others think too highly of themselves to "stoop" to saying thank you.

Learn to show appreciation for everything—big or small—and develop an attitude of gratitude. It's wrong to be so unthankful. God has given you physical life, and followers of Jesus have been given eternal life. No one *deserves* anything. Everything in life is a gift to be appreciated.

WHAT'S A GIRL TO DO?

Which girls are showing the trait of being unthankful?

- ☐ As Mira walks into school, a teacher holds the door for her, but Mira says nothing as she passes through.
- ☐ Rose sits down to a mouthwatering piece of strawberry shortcake and says, "Thanks, Mom!"
- ☐ Libby is dropped off at school by her big sister. She hops out of the car, saying, "See ya!"

CONNECTING TO GOD

Dear Lord, I don't mean to be unthankful. Please open my eyes and help me to notice when others do things for me. Amen.

more to explore

One of them, when he saw that he was healed, returned, and with a loud voice glorified God, and fell down on his face at His feet, giving Him thanks ... So Jesus answered and said, "Were there not ten cleansed? But where are the [other] nine?"
—Luke 17:15–17 (NKJV)

devotion 80

LORD, accept my offering of praise and teach me
your regulations.

—Psalm 119:108 (NLT)

You're sick with a wretched stomach virus for five days, but
finally on day six you feel better. Your stomach no longer
heaves, and your head has stopped pounding. "Oh, thank
you, Lord!" you say, grateful to be up and around again. You
shuffle to the back porch and collapse in the swing, enjoying
the chirping wrens and gentle breeze blowing through the
aspen trees. Your mom brings you a glass of orange juice.
"Would you like me to fix you a poached egg?" she asks.
"Maybe, in a minute." You lean your head on your mom's
shoulder. "Thanks for all the private nursing this week," you
say. Your mom smiles and replies, "You're worth it."

Someone who is grateful is thankful for things—big
and small. She shows appreciation to others for the good
things said to her and done for her. "Thank you" is something she says often—and means it. A grateful person
doesn't behave as if people owe her special treatment. She
considers the sacrifices others make for her. She is first
and foremost grateful to God.

Too often we focus on the sacrifices *we* make for
others—what *we* have to tolerate or how much *we* help.

Much less time is spent considering the sacrifices others make for us: buying things for us, listening to us, taking us places, cooking or doing laundry for us. Each of these things takes time from someone's busy schedule. Be alert to such sacrifices—and don't forget to say "thank you."

WHAT'S A GIRL TO DO?

Which girl is showing the trait of being grateful?

- ☐ When the security employee at the hockey rink returns her missing jacket, Mira says, "It's about time."
- ☐ Becky climbs into the minivan at the theater and says, "Thanks for picking me up."
- ☐ When Kayla finds her clean clothes folded and laid on her bed, she wonders, *Can't Mom ever put my stuff away?*

CONNECTING TO GOD

Dear Lord, forgive me for not noticing when people help me out. I want my friends and family to know how much I appreciate them. Amen.

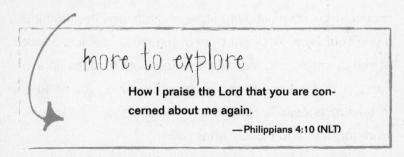

more to explore

How I praise the Lord that you are concerned about me again.

—Philippians 4:10 (NLT)

God is not a God of disorder but of peace.

—1 Corinthians 14:33 (TNIV)

Grace loved sports of all kinds: swimming, softball, in-line skating, biking, and hiking. She had a never-ending supply of energy. Unfortunately, Grace's energy never quite lasted long enough to put away her equipment. Her parents and sisters constantly tripped over her skates and bike left in the driveway, softballs on the stairs, and hiking boots on the back porch. Her wet bathing suit and towel landed on the bathroom floor. Grace had always been messy, claiming she had much more important—and fun—things to do than to "be a neat freak."

A messy person leaves disorder wherever she goes. Her locker is littered, her bedroom is cluttered, her bathroom ranges from untidy to filthy, and (usually) her thoughts are in confusion. At the bottom of the messy habit is a lack of self-discipline and laziness. It takes work to clean up a mess or prevent one from occurring. However, you need to take responsibility for your own belongings. It's a lot of work for others to pick up after you.

Self-discipline (or self-control) is a fruit of the Spirit, so pray for help! Using willpower to overcome a messy habit won't work for long. Instead, ask for God's power in your situation. Bit by bit, he can help you form good habits and bring order out of your disorder. You'll be amazed at how much calmer you'll feel inside as your surroundings become neat and organized.

WHAT'S A GIRL TO DO?

Which girls are showing the trait of being messy?

- ☐ Kayla can clean her room in ten minutes flat because most of the mess on the floor gets shoved under the bed.
- ☐ Libby can clean her room in ten minutes flat because she picks up her mess every morning before school and again before bedtime.
- ☐ Rose can clean her room in ten minutes flat by skimming over the surface of the mess, picking up just enough so that her mom won't yell at her.

CONNECTING TO GOD

Dear Lord, forgive me for not taking better care of my things. Help me to be more responsible. Amen.

more to explore

You shall set them in two rows, six in a row, on the pure gold table before the LORD ... Every Sabbath he shall set it in order before the LORD continually.

—Leviticus 24:6, 8 (NKJV)

... TO ORGANIZED

**She carefully watches everything in her household
and suffers nothing from laziness.**

—Proverbs 31:27 (NLT)

Twice a month you volunteer in the toddler room of the
church nursery. You rush in as church starts to set out the
cookies and pour the tiny cups of fruit drink. You wipe runny
noses, break up fights, and take toddlers to the bathroom.
No job gets quite finished before you're needed for something else. Every week your head aches before the hour is
over, and you wish you'd never volunteered to help. One
Sunday, you decide to get organized. You arrive ten minutes early to get everything ready. You greet every child
and parent when they come in. You take each thing one at a
time with a calm attitude. It is still busy, but you feel like you
are on top of things, and you have a good time. An organized person plans ahead and knows how she will handle
unexpected situations. She develop methods that work for
her—ways to keep her life from becoming unmanageable.

Yes, being organized is more work than being messy or
haphazard. More work at *first*, anyway. But the payoffs are
huge. You enjoy your work and home more—and others
enjoy *you* more. You avoid many crises because you stop
misplacing important items. Try organizing your room, your

desk, and your homework for a month. See if you enjoy the peace even more than the mess.

WHAT'S A GIRL TO DO?

Which girls are showing the trait of organization?

☐ Becky gets the kids in her neighborhood together and divides them into groups to go door-to-door, collecting canned goods for hurricane victims.

☐ Cassie packs for vacation two days early, finding small containers for her art supplies, her candy, her books, and her camera equipment.

☐ Mira checks out six books from the public library. She reads them in the car, her room, at school, and outdoors. On the due date, she can only find three books.

CONNECTING TO GOD

Dear Lord, thank you for providing us with an orderly world, where everything works together in amazing harmony. Please help me to be orderly. Amen.

more to explore

"You shall select from all the people able men, ... and place such over them to be rulers of thousands, rulers of hundreds, rulers of fifties, and rulers of tens ... So it will be easier for you, for they will bear the burden with you."

—Exodus 18:21–22 (NKJV)

FROM LAZY . . .

Lazy people want much but get little.

—Proverbs 13:4 (NLT)

Olivia loved school—at least the social part. When her social studies group was assigned England for their project, Olivia reluctantly joined the others after school for a planning session. She spent her time writing notes to her best friend instead of paying attention. The chairman of their group sent her emails several times per week, which Olivia deleted. When asked at school, she assured the group she was working hard on her part—Britain's commerce—although she hadn't actually opened any of the books she'd checked out. There was plenty of time for that later! However, in the end she was disappointed in her personal grade. The group did well as a whole, but Olivia's report (written at the last minute) earned a D. Her grade matched the effort she'd put into it.

A person who is lazy is unwilling to work. A lazy girl prefers idleness and lying around. She's unmotivated and is sometimes said to be "allergic to work." In truth, she simply doesn't like to work and doesn't push herself to get busy or to help others. The Bible actually calls a lazy servant "wicked" (Matthew 25:26).

Being lazy seems more fun at the moment than working, and, to be honest, it often *is* more fun! But the consequences — like poor grades, gaining too much weight, and no income — are definitely *not* fun. And if others are depending on you for promised help, being lazy can cost you a few friends.

WHAT'S A GIRL TO DO?

Which girl is showing the trait of being lazy?

- ☐ Rose waits until she smells food already cooking before asking her mom if there's anything she can do to help with supper.
- ☐ Mira signs up to help clean the city park and shows up early to start work.
- ☐ Cassie eats her lunch on time, throws away the trash from the table, and then has time to chat with her friends before class.

CONNECTING TO GOD

Dear Lord, forgive me for the times I've given in to laziness. Give me real joy in being active and productive. Amen.

more to explore

Those too lazy to plow in the right season will have no food at the harvest.
—Proverbs 20:4 (NLT)

She was always doing good and helping the poor.
—Acts 9:36 (TNIV)

You walk into the kitchen after school and discover one of
the dirtiest children you've ever laid eyes on seated at the
table with your little brother. "This is Tim," your brother
says. "He moved in across the street with his grandparents
over the weekend." You're surprised, as the grandparents
are really old and in poor health. You plop down at the table
and join them as they have a snack of peanut butter on
crackers and chocolate milk.

The boys have spelling homework. While your brother
is a so-so speller, you notice that Tim is very poor at it.
They both need help, and spelling happens to be your
strength. (You won the citywide spelling bee twice.) Even
more, you suspect Tim needs kindness. The first few times
you work with them after school, Tim never glances up
from his page and won't look you in the eye. By the third
week, though, he can spell all his words. He also finally
takes a peek at you—and grins.

A person who is helpful likes to be of service. She
lends a hand to anyone needing assistance. A helpful person is happy to do favors and pitch in to finish chores and

projects. Followers of Jesus are usually helpful. In fact, one name for the Holy Spirit is Helper.

Being helpful requires time and energy. It takes noticing the needs of others and being willing to do something about them. One of the most helpful things you can do for others, which also takes time and energy, is to pray for them.

WHAT'S A GIRL TO DO?

Which girl is showing the trait of being helpful?

☐ Kayla steps over several towels on the floor in the bathroom without picking them up.

☐ Libby can see how tired her mom looks while folding the family's laundry. Libby feels sorry for her mom.

☐ When she sees her older neighbor taking several slow trips out to the car to bring groceries into the house, Rose runs over to help her.

CONNECTING TO GOD

Dear Lord, thank you for never being too busy to help me. Create in me a helpful heart for others too. Amen.

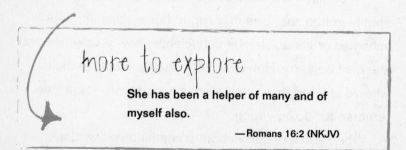

more to explore

She has been a helper of many and of myself also.

—Romans 16:2 (NKJV)

FROM GUILTY ...

The person who keeps all of the laws except one is as guilty as the person who has broken all of God's laws.
—James 2:10 (NLT)

After Kimberly's dad died, she and her mom were more like best friends than mother and daughter. When her mom remarried and Kimberly inherited a younger stepsister, it was a huge change. Often she longed for the days when she and her mom could sit for hours and talk. One day, while Kimberly told her mom about a girl at school who bullied her, Kimberly's stepsister wandered into the living room. Frustrated, Kimberly snapped at her and said, "Go away! Why do you have to barge in where you're not wanted?" The little girl ran off in tears. Guilt washed over Kimberly like a flood.

When a person feels guilty, she feels responsible for some wrongdoing. She may regret her actions and feel ashamed or sheepish. Her conscience may trouble her, and she may be sorry. However, some guilty people—those who've ignored their consciences a long time—feel little remorse for doing wrong.

When you feel guilty about something you've done and want to make things right with God, go to the Father in prayer, admit the wrong action, and be forgiven. "If we confess our sins, He is faithful and just to forgive us our sins and to cleanse us from all unrighteousness" (1 John 1:9 NKJV).

WHAT'S A GIRL TO DO?

Which girl is showing the trait of feeling guilty?

☐ Rose doesn't have her homework done and refuses to look up from her desk or meet her teacher's eye.

☐ Caroline takes some money from her mom's purse, sticks it in her pocket, and goes whistling out the door.

☐ Mira snaps at her best friend, gives her a nasty stare, and then turns and stomps away.

CONNECTING TO GOD

Dear Lord, I do wrong things every day—some big and some little. Help me use the guilty feeling to turn to you. Amen.

more to explore

Christ has rescued us from the curse pronounced by the law. When he was hung on the cross, he took upon himself the curse for our wrongdoing.

—Galatians 3:13 (NLT)

... TO CLEANSED

**Who dares accuse us whom God has chosen for his
own? No one—for God himself has given us right
standing with himself.**

—Romans 8:33 (NLT)

Your family has a computer, but there are certain rules you
promise to follow when using it. One rule is that you must
stay out of chat rooms. Then your best friend finds a teen
chat room for Christians. What could be wrong with that?
So after school, you go to the site, set up an account,
and begin chatting. It's okay, but not as much fun as you'd
expected. Although you could erase the website from the
computer history, there's no need. Your parents trust you
and probably won't check up on you. That whole week the
knowledge that you broke their trust eats at you. Finally,
on Friday night you confess about the chat room and say
you're sorry. Your parents are disappointed, but glad you
told them. You sleep well that night for the first time all
week.

To be cleansed (or cleaned) is to be spotless and
washed fresh. For a believer, being cleansed means being
forgiven—becoming pure and sinless in God's sight. We
can be cleansed because Jesus died on the cross for our
sins, making a way for us to be joined again with God.

As the Bible says, "Wash me, and I shall be whiter than snow" (Psalm 51:7 NKJV).

We continue in a cleansed state when we talk to God each day and confess the wrong things we've said or done. There's nothing like the peace of a clean conscience!

WHAT'S A GIRL TO DO?

Which girl is showing the trait of being cleansed?

- ☐ Cassie feels excited when the clerk gives her too much change.
- ☐ Becky breaks a dish accidentally and apologizes to her grandmother about it.
- ☐ Kayla doesn't finish her homework and tells the teacher she lost her paper.

CONNECTING TO GOD

Dear Lord, I'd like to be more sensitive to the times when I do something wrong. Please help me to confess my sins. Amen.

more to explore

There is no condemnation for those who belong to Christ Jesus. ... The power of the life-giving Spirit has freed you from the power of sin that leads to death.

—Romans 8:1–2 (NLT)

devotion 87

> "They will throw their money in the streets, tossing it out like worthless trash ... Their love of money made them stumble into sin. They were proud of their beautiful jewelry."
>
> —Ezekiel 7:19–20 (NLT)

For her birthday, Whitney's grandparents gave her a hundred dollars. Her parents wanted her to save most of it for college. Whitney considered the idea for a week. Then on Saturday she met her friend at the mall. There she spent the money on a pair of designer jeans and a ball cap with an expensive logo. She had enough change left over to buy ice cream for her friend and herself. As she expected, her parents were upset with her decision. *Oh well*, Whitney thought, *it's my birthday money.*

Someone who is extravagant is excessive and wasteful in her spending. An extravagant girl shows little restraint, and her spending habits are extreme. Often extravagant spenders like to show off what they've bought. They receive much of their self-esteem from the amount of money something costs. Extravagant spenders rarely consider how their money might be used to benefit someone else.

Buying nice things if you can afford them isn't a sin, nor is having plenty of money. But being wasteful with what

God gives you *is* wrong. Before making a big purchase or buying some expensive designer clothing, ask yourself why you want to do this. Pray also. Ask the Lord how he would prefer to have you spend the money.

WHAT'S A GIRL TO DO?

Which girl is showing the trait of being extravagant?

- ☐ Libby takes the earnings from her summer job and buys school clothes with half of it and saves the rest.
- ☐ Rose cleans out her savings account to redecorate her bedroom with new furniture, new drapes, and new pictures.
- ☐ Mira wants to buy a DVD, but she decides to check it out from the public library, instead, for free.

CONNECTING TO GOD

Dear Lord, help me to stop and think before I spend my money wastefully or for wrong reasons. I want to be responsible with my money. Amen.

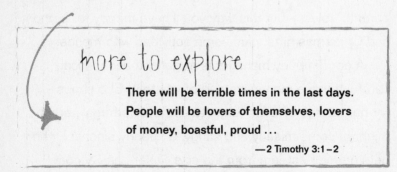

more to explore

There will be terrible times in the last days. People will be lovers of themselves, lovers of money, boastful, proud ...

—2 Timothy 3:1–2

"The servant who received the five bags of silver
began to invest the money and earned five more."

—Matthew 25:16 (NLT)

You get a job detassling corn during the summer on your
uncle's farm. Although it's hot, exhausting work, you're able
to keep up. You save your paychecks, spending only small
sums each week on food and drink to take with you to the
field. At the end of the summer, the seed corn company
gives your crew a bonus for doing a great job and finishing
early. Your share of the bonus is nearly two hundred dollars. You give twenty dollars to a fund-raiser at your church.
Twenty-eight dollars gets your bike repaired. The rest goes
into the bank. You can't hold a job during the school year—
parents' rules—but this way you'll have money for birthday
and Christmas gifts, plus some activities with friends.

A good money manager is frugal and economical,
careful to save money instead of waste it. She shops
for bargains. However, taken to extreme, a frugal person
might become miserly and stingy, a "penny-pincher" who
gets her self-esteem from the size of her bank account.
But when in balance, an economical person is a very good
manager of her money.

Being a good money manager means taking care of the wealth God has entrusted to you. He wants you to spend, save, and give it away wisely. Giving to God's work (like at church or a Christian organization) is important. So is saving money for emergencies. A warning—don't put your trust in your bank account instead of God. *He* is your security—not your money.

WHAT'S A GIRL TO DO?

Which girl is showing the trait of being a good money manager?

- ☐ Becky takes a month's worth of allowance and spends it at a water park in one day.
- ☐ Cassie accepts a Saturday babysitting job for six weeks to earn money for a band trip.
- ☐ Kayla borrows money from her friend so she can go to the movies. She promises to pay her back next week when she gets her allowance.

CONNECTING TO GOD

Dear Lord, sometimes I make poor decisions about spending money. Help me to remember to stop and pray first. Amen.

---

more to explore

Wisdom and money can get you almost anything, but only wisdom can save your life.

—Ecclesiastes 7:12 (NLT)

Blessing and cursing come pouring out of the same mouth. Surely, my brothers and sisters, this is not right!

—James 3:10 (NLT)

Erica didn't swear, but her friends had picked up some nasty words over the summer. At first Erica found the language disgusting. Inwardly she cringed, while outwardly she laughed along with the others. Over time, she stopped being shocked. In fact, she sprinkled her own conversation with a few four-letter words. Erica cleaned up her language at home and at church, careful to save her cusswords for her friends. Sometimes she felt guilty. Being two separate people didn't seem right somehow—and she began to wonder which girl was the real Erica.

A person with the trait of cursing uses profanity, or "gutter language" to liven up her speech. Four-letter words and obscenities have no place in the believer's vocabulary. Words are powerful and can be incredibly destructive (to yourself and others) if used for cursing.

In order to break the habit of using cusswords and obscene language, you may have to do two things. First, it may be necessary to find new friends. Hang around people at school and church who don't talk that way. Second, you need to clean out your mind and fill it with godly thinking. Your words come directly from your thoughts. And your thoughts are influenced by the books you read, the music you listen to, and the movies you watch. "Fix your thoughts on what is true, and honorable, and right, and pure, and lovely, and admirable. Think about things that are excellent and worthy of praise" (Philippians 4:8 NLT). Then what comes out of your mouth will be pleasing to God—and to you again.

WHAT'S A GIRL TO DO?

Which girls are showing the trait of cursing?

- ☐ Rose stubs her toe in the night and swears under her breath.
- ☐ Mira is irritated at her mom and calls her a nasty name.
- ☐ Cassie spills her milk at supper, reaches for a paper towel, and says, "Oh well!"

CONNECTING TO GOD

Dear Lord, I don't want to have a gutter mouth. Help me choose words pleasing to you! Amen.

more to explore

As he loved cursing, so let it come to him; as he did not delight in blessing, so let it be far from him.

—Psalm 109:17 (NKJV)

... TO BLESSING

**Bless those who persecute you; bless and do
not curse.**

—Romans 12:14 (TNIV)

Your older sister has been difficult to live with since her
boyfriend decided to date someone else. She snaps at
you for no good reason and rudely cuts you off if you ask
a question. At first you snap right back at her. After all, it's
not your fault her boyfriend likes someone else. You're only
trying to get along! One Sunday, the sermon is about blessing those who persecute you, and it makes you think. The
next time she's rude, you tell her you're sorry she's having
a rough time. You add that whether her boyfriend appreci-
ates her or not, she's beautiful and talented and the best
sister a girl could have. She's shocked, but tears fill her
eyes as she gives you a hug.

A person with the habit of blessing declares that others
are special and gifted. To bless someone means to wish
them good fortune and favor and to pray that things go well
with them.

You can bless someone whether or not they deserve
it. The Lord does it for us all the time! Blessing others can
become a habit in the same way cursing can—but with

such different results. Try it today. Instead of being negative when someone deserves it, try blessing them instead. What a difference it makes, both in them and in your own attitude.

WHAT'S A GIRL TO DO?

Which girls are showing the trait of blessing?

- ☐ The boy who sits behind Cassie keeps tapping her desk with his foot, and she rolls her eyes in annoyance.
- ☐ When Becky's neighbor yells at her to keep her puppy out of her flower bed, she replies, "I will. I don't want him to hurt your beautiful roses."
- ☐ Kayla's friend forgets to call her Tuesday night. On Wednesday, Kayla kindly tells her that she missed talking to her the night before.

CONNECTING TO GOD

Dear Lord, help me remember how much grace you give me. Help me to bless others too. Amen.

more to explore

Do not repay evil with evil or insult with insult. On the contrary, repay evil with blessing, because to this you were called so that you may inherit a blessing.

—1 Peter 3:9 (TNIV)

faiThGirLz!

Faithgirlz!–Inner Beauty, Outward Faith

Sophie Series

Written by Nancy Rue

Meet Sophie LaCroix, a creative soul who's destined to become a great film director someday. But many times, her overactive imagination gets her in trouble!

Book 1: *Sophie's World*
Softcover, ISBN 0-310-70756-0

Book 2: *Sophie's Secret*
Softcover, ISBN 0-310-70757-9

Book 3: *Sophie and the Scoundrels*
Softcover, ISBN 0-310-70758-7

Book 4: *Sophie's Irish Showdown*
Softcover, ISBN 0-310-70759-5

Book 5: *Sophie's First Dance?*
Softcover, ISBN 0-310-70760-9

Book 6: *Sophie's Stormy Summer*
Softcover, ISBN 0-310-70761-7

Book 7: *Sophie Breaks the Code*
Softcover, ISBN 0-310-71022-7

Book 8: *Sophie Tracks a Thief*
Softcover, ISBN 0-310-71023-5

Book 9: *Sophie Flakes Out*
Softcover, ISBN 0-310-71024-3

Book 10: *Sophie Loves Jimmy*
Softcover, ISBN 0-310-71025-1

Book 11: *Sophie Loses the Lead*
Softcover, ISBN 0-310-71026-X

Book 12: *Sophie's Encore*
Softcover, ISBN 0-310-71027-8

Available at your local bookstore!
Visit faithgirlz.com; it's the place for girls ages 8-12.

faiThGirLz!

Faithgirlz!–Inner Beauty, Outward Faith

Everybody Tells Me to Be Myself but I Don't Know Who I Am

This new addition to the Faithgirlz! line helps girls face the challenges of being their true selves with fun activities, interactive text, and insightful tips.

Softcover, ISBN 0-310-71295-5

Girl Politics

Parents and kids alike may think that getting teased or arguing with friends is just part of growing up, but where is the line between normal kid stuff and harmful behavior? This book is a guide for girls on how to deal with girl politics, God-style.

Softcover, ISBN 0-310-71296-3

Beauty Lab

Beauty tips and the secret of true inner beauty are revealed in this interactive, inspirational, fun addition to the Faithgirlz! line

Softcover, ISBN 0-310-71276-9

Body Talk

In a world where bodies are commodities, girls are under more pressure at younger ages. This book is a fun and God-centered way to give girls the facts and self-confidence they need as they mature into young women.

Softcover, ISBN 0-310-71275-0

Available at your local bookstore!

faiThGirLz!

Faithgirlz!–Inner Beauty, Outward Faith

No Boys Allowed
Devotions for Girls
Written by Kristi Holl

This short, ninety-day devotional for girls ages 10 and up is written in an upbeat, lively, funny, and tween-friendly way, incorporating the graphic, fast-moving feel of a teen magazine.

Softcover, ISBN 0-310-70718-8

Girlz Rock
Devotions for You
Written by Kristi Holl

In this ninety-day devotional, devotions like "Who Am I?" help pave the spiritual walk of life, and the "Girl Talk" feature poses questions that really bring each message home. No matter how bad things get, you can always count on God.

Softcover, ISBN 0-310-70899-0

Chick Chat
More Devotions for Girls
Written by Kristi Holl

This ninety-day devotional brings the Bible right into your world and offers lots to learn and think about.

Softcover, ISBN 0-310-71143-6

Shine On, Girl!
Devotions to Keep You Sparkling
Written by Kristi Holl

This ninety-day devotional will "totally" help teen girls connect with God, as well as learn his will for their lives.

Softcover, ISBN 0-310-71144-4

Available at your local bookstore!

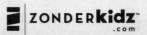

faiThGirLz!

Faithgirlz!–Inner Beauty, Outward Faith

My Faithgirlz! Journal
This Girl Rocks!

The questions in this new Faithgirlz! journal focus on your life, family, friends, and future. Because your favorites and issues seem to change every day, the same set of questions are repeated in each section. Includes quizzes to promote reflection and stickers to add fun!

My Faithgirlz! Journal
Spiral, ISBN 0-310-71190-8

NIV Faithgirlz! Backpack Bible

The full NIV text in a handy size for girls on the go—for ages 8 and up.

NIV Faithgirlz! Backpack Bible
Periwinkle Italian Duo-Tone™
ISBN 0-310-71012-X

Available at your local bookstore!

visit faiThGirLz.com
Inner beauty, outward faith

Faithgirlz!™ is based on 2 Corinthians 4:38—So we fix our eyes not on what is seen, but on what is unseen. For what is seen is temporary, but what is unseen is eternal (NIV)—and helps girls find Inner Beauty, Outward Faith.

Every girl wants to know she's totally unique and special. This Bible says that with Faithgirlz! sparkle! Now girls can grow closer to God as they discover the journey of a lifetime, in their language, for their world.

The NIV Faithgirlz! Bible

Hardcover • ISBN 0-310-71581-4

Softcover • ISBN 0-310-71582-2

The NIV Faithgirlz! Bible

Italian Duo-Tone™ • ISBN 0-310-71583-0

We want to hear from you. Please send your comments about this book to us in care of zreview@zondervan.com. Thank you.

ZONDERkidz™
.com

ZONDERVAN.com/
AUTHORTRACKER
follow your favorite authors